THE UNFOLDING
NOW

BOOKS BY A. H. ALMAAS

Essence with The Elixir of Enlightenment: The Diamond
Approach to Inner Realization

Facets of Unity: The Enneagram of Holy Ideas

The Inner Journey Home: Soul's Realization of the
Unity of Reality

Luminous Night's Journey: An Autobiographical Fragment

DIAMOND MIND SERIES

VOLUME 1. The Void: Inner Spaciousness and Ego Structure

VOLUME 2. The Pearl Beyond Price: Integration of Personality
into Being: An Object Relations Approach

VOLUME 3. The Point of Existence: Transformations
of Narcissism in Self-Realization

DIAMOND HEART SERIES

BOOK ONE. Elements of the Real in Man

BOOK TWO. The Freedom to Be

BOOK THREE. Being and the Meaning of Life

BOOK FOUR. Indestructible Innocence

DIAMOND BODY SERIES

Spacecruiser Inquiry: True Guidance for the Inner Journey

Brilliancy: The Essence of Intelligence

The Unfolding Now: Realizing Your True Nature through
the Practice of Presence

For more information on A. H. Almaas and all of his
publications, please go to www.ahalmaas.com.

THE UNFOLDING
NOW

Realizing Your
True Nature
through the
Practice of Presence

A. H. ALMAAS

SHAMBHALA
BOSTON & LONDON 2008

Shambhala Publications, Inc.
Horticultural Hall
300 Massachusetts Avenue
Boston, Massachusetts 02115
www.shambhala.com

9 8 7 6 5 4 3 2

Printed in the United States of America

♾ This edition is printed on acid-free paper that meets the
American National Standards Institute z39.48 Standard.
♻ This book was printed on 30% postconsumer recycled paper.
For more information please visit us at www.shambhala.com.
Distributed in the United States by Random House, Inc.,
and in Canada by Random House of Canada Ltd

Designed by Dede Cummings Design

Library of Congress Cataloging-in-Publication Data
Almaas, A. H.
The unfolding now: realizing your true nature through the
practice of presence / A. H. Almaas.—1st ed.
p.   cm.—(Diamond Body Series; 3)
Includes index.
ISBN 978-1-59030-559-1 (pbk.: alk. paper)
1. Attention. 2. Self. I. Title.
BF321.A46 2008
153.7'5—dc22
2007042699

Dedicated to all the students of the Diamond Approach:

BY LEARNING TO VALUE and appreciate experiencing, knowing, and accepting where you truly are, you give our human potential the opportunity to deepen and soar to heights that humanity greatly needs. It has always been an inspiration for me to see how, by sincerely following a genuine teaching, you provide an opening for reality to reveal its perfections and hence offer the world a glimpse of the harmony possible for it.

Contents

Editor's Preface

THE HIDDEN RICHNESS THAT rests in our life, in our heart, in our experience is *here*—not *over there*, in some better life, in some other house, in some other career, in some other relationship or country or spiritual school. One time, perhaps, we actually knew that—and then we forgot. From time to time, we are reminded by others of that richness, or we rediscover it ourselves. But over and over, we forget.

When we lose touch with the fullness of who we really are, when we ourselves cannot recognize or appreciate it, when it is invisible to us or seems inaccessible, the knowledge that we are the location and source of what we are seeking is only abstract information, irrelevant to our personal situation. It cannot affect who we are or how we live if we can't find this richness in our immediate experience, can't feel it or taste it or sense it directly. In fact, what we find is that most everything in our life works against our turning that knowledge into the currency of personal inner richness.

Our beliefs about what will allow us to survive, or what can help us solve our problems, or what will make us happy, or even what will fulfill our desire to make a difference in the world all seem to point us away from *here*. We are always going somewhere, internally or externally—to the store, the movies, the beach, the office, the restaurant, the television, the Internet, the newspaper, the latest spiritual teacher to come to town, our partners, our children, our friends, our parents, our worries, our concerns, our fears, our hopes. And on and on. We are in motion, going after, seeking out, restless, never satisfied, never at peace.

This seems to be the central dilemma of human life—that it is easier to desire what is *over there* than to appreciate what is *right here*. In fact, what is here seems to be so fundamentally inferior, less than, or inadequate compared to what is apparently over there, that it hardly seems worth the effort to look here. Why not just go over there?

Why, indeed? All spiritual paths, traditions, and schools have been attempting to answer that question for us for thousands of years. Each in their own way teaches that your spirit or your soul—your original unconditioned consciousness—exists only in you, so going elsewhere can never give you access to your essential nature, to who you really are. And the essence that is *you* is purported to be something quite magnificent: Your true spiritual nature is said to be full of love, peace, strength, beauty, joy, compassion, wisdom, and intelligence.

But even imagining yourself with this spiritual nature immediately conjures up the belief that you can only find these qualities somewhere else. After all, it is not what you experience in yourself now, right? You're not there . . . yet. Spiritual paths and techniques thus become ways of getting *there*—to the place where you feel real, where you will become all these wonderful things. So you meditate, attempting to empty your mind or calm yourself or focus on an image or let go of all attachment. Or you chant and dance to invoke your spirit. Or you say prayers and go on vision quests. Yet all these techniques of finding your deeper self subtly imply that where you are now in yourself is not where you need to be.

You are seeking some ideal of the spiritual self and using these methods to attempt to reach that. The result is that the spiritual search can evoke the same dilemma that all other aspects of your life do. Since you cannot feel anything essential or profound in your present experience, you must travel away from here to find what you are looking for—even if it's your own True Nature.

What if you found a spiritual method that focused completely on being right here? What if it did not require you to change yourself in any way in order to find yourself? What if you didn't have to go away from yourself in order to go deeper? What if you could stop comparing yourself to something or someone that you imagine to be better or truer or more spiritual? What if transformation were a natural, spontaneous process that occurs only when you stop being so busy trying to change yourself?

The Unfolding Now is an introduction and invitation to just such a path. A. H. Almaas, the founder of the Diamond Approach® to inner realization, presents a progressive unfoldment of understanding what it means to "be where you are."

Though being where you are may seem equivalent to stopping the search or seeing through the self or waking up to the oneness of reality, the path of the Diamond Approach is distinctly different from the Advaita paths of spiritual realization. These approaches invite one to directly see through the false identities of self in order to recognize and be the oneness of reality. Almaas's approach is not a sudden awakening or a confrontational breakthrough but a gradual and gentle unfoldment of the realization of our True Nature. This subtle realization is not a single state but includes myriad possibilities—including the state of oneness.

In one sense, it is the simplest possible experience to be as you are in this moment without any inner movement away from yourself, without any judgment or reaction, without any explanation or justification, without any longing or seeking after something else. However, what Almaas does is reveal how multifaceted this simplicity of being actually is. We do not generally appreciate why the simple act of being is so difficult and why it challenges so much in our familiar sense of ourselves. In particular, it confronts the belief that becoming more real, more truly who we are, can only happen through our own intervention. But it is because of this very belief that we are always leaving ourselves. It is also why we believe that our spiritual development requires great effort and achievement.

This book offers a welcome alternative to all that struggle: a way to honor yourself where you are, how you are, and who you are, without judgment and without comparison to any standard.

To be where you are does not mean adopting a particular spiritual posture, such as clarity and equanimity, or an open-hearted stance of compassion and love. To be where you are means just that: to be where you are. Exactly where you are—warts and all, as the saying goes. But it also means becoming aware of where that is—aware in a way that is open, respectful, curious, and welcoming.

It is this process of opening to where you are that Almaas invites and encourages with great compassion and directness. He reveals many of the specific barriers to this allowing awareness and natural appreciation of wherever it is that we find ourselves. And he shows how, as the barriers are recognized, we can begin to see the ignorance implicit in them. This ignorance—that which we simply are not aware of—has set in place and maintained many of our beliefs about ourselves and reality. As that ignorance gives way to understanding, the barriers become less solid and fixed. Our knowing of where we are grows.

In this way, the teaching gently awakens in us the preciousness of what it means to leave ourselves alone, what it means to stop all of our subtle and constant inner activity of messing with ourselves. We can taste how deeply relaxed and at rest we feel when we don't try to direct or manipulate our experience in any way. And we can also feel our resistance to that relaxation based on a deep fear of becoming passive, dependent, or helpless about our life.

Our relaxation into exactly who and where we are is what allows us to stop defending and hiding who we truly are. In the restfulness, we can simply be—be with awareness and awakeness and aliveness. This is something quite different from the passivity we feared. In simply being, we discover the implicit nature of Being, of *our* Being. We find that this Being is dynamic and intelligent. It becomes the agent of change—transforming our consciousness by revealing deeper and deeper truth. In this process, we begin to taste flavors and qualities of our True Nature, our essence.

This is the perennial wisdom: who we truly are is always right here, hidden within our experience, waiting to reveal itself. And this revelation is available and will happen if we are willing to open to what it truly means to be where we are. If we give ourselves the gift of not going anywhere, not trying to do anything, and not looking elsewhere, we step into the very real possibility of knowing the essence of who we are. This core principle underlies the practice of inquiry, the primary method of the Diamond Approach. The teaching presented in this book elucidates this principle and its profound relevance for living a satisfying human life.

The Unfolding Now is based on transcripts of a summer retreat given by Almaas for the members of his spiritual school. The presentation has been modified from its original format so that it communicates more clearly on the printed page, while retaining the experiential component of inquiries into the material that the students engaged in.

This component is in the form of exploration sessions at the end of each chapter. These reflections and questions provide guidance to help you absorb the subject matter in a more direct, personal way. We suggest that you enter into these exercises with as much curiosity, openness, and willingness as you can.

I leave you with an old Sufi story. It illuminates the basic misconception that creates the need for the inner journey Almaas describes in this book.

Someone saw Nasrudin searching for something on the ground.

"What have you lost, Mulla?" he asked.

"My key," said the Mulla. So they both went down on their knees and looked for it.

After a time the other man said, "Where exactly did you drop it?"

"In my own house."

"Then why are you looking here?"

"There is more light here than inside my own house."
— IDRIES SHAH
The Exploits of the Incomparable Mulla Nasrudin

The Unfolding Now invites us to bring light inside our own house so
we can find what we have lost touch with in ourselves.

BYRON BROWN

Note to the Reader

THE UNFOLDING NOW is an introduction to a spiritual path that is based on being with your own immediate experience in an intimate and curious way. It is not about doing anything to your experience, but neither is it simply detaching from your experience. The spiritual practice that facilitates and supports being with your experience is what we call inquiry. Inquiry is based on an open and curious desire for knowing the truth of your experience exactly as it is. This truth is inherent in each moment of your experience and therefore a sincere interest in discovering it will invite that truth to reveal itself.

The way Almaas presents this teaching is itself an invitation to do inquiry. So feel free to stop at any time and explore within your own experience whatever he is describing. To help you focus your explorations, specific suggestions for inquiry are included in the text. At the end of each chapter, an Exploration Session will specify an area of inquiry related to the subject matter to guide your exploration and the development of your capacities for this practice. You are encouraged to do these inquiry exercises either alone through journaling or verbally with fellow explorers.

If you choose the first approach—writing out your answers in a journal—it is good to allow between fifteen and thirty minutes for each exercise. This will provide time for the questions to sit a while, bringing up responses from deeper in your consciousness rather than simply what is most readily available. Don't worry about writing style or grammar or spelling—what's important is to allow all of your thoughts and feelings and awarenesses to flow out and be articulated. This will make room for insights and recognitions to emerge about what you have written and for your experience to continue to unfold.

If you choose to do the exercises with someone else, generally it is good to plan on an hour of time to explore together, but it could be less if need be. You can use the simple format of taking fifteen to twenty minutes each to do the exercise. While one person inquires, the other is a silent witness who is practicing being present to his or her own experience while listening in an open, curious way to the inquiry. This is a particular benefit of exploring with others: your own inquiry process will be deepened by witnessing another inquiring. It is also good to allow time to discuss together the inquiry process and what you have discovered by doing it.

Should you find yourself especially interested in the inquiry practice itself beyond the exercises presented in this book, you are encouraged to read *Spacecruiser Inquiry: True Guidance for the Inner Journey* by A. H. Almaas (2002).

Inquiry is a spiritual practice, and like any other, it develops over time. Reading and rereading this book as you follow the gradual unfolding of your inner life can support and enrich the depth and subtlety of your inner journey. Finding your own rhythm and pace of opening will thus allow inquiry to reveal the hidden richness of your Being.

Acknowledgments

THIS BOOK BEGAN AS A TEACHING retreat that I conducted during the summer of 2003 in Sacramento, California, for experienced students in the Ridhwan School. I intended it to be a simple and direct guidance on how to work on oneself, how to meditate, and how to explore one's reality and the reality of the world. By the end of the retreat, many students had expressed their wish that this teaching be put in written form. Many thought it could be a readable, approachable book for a larger audience beyond members of the School, even though it deals with profound matters.

I liked the idea, saw the point they were making, and discussed it with Byron Brown, my chief editor. He agreed that it would be a valuable support for traversing the inner spiritual path and one that could speak to people who are not familiar with the teaching of the Diamond Approach. He asked Elianne Obadia, whom he had supervised on other projects, to do the primary editing and worked with her to turn the transcripts of the talks and meetings into chapters with practice exercises. Elianne, with Byron's guidance, did a wonderful job in transforming my talks into good, readable prose. And Damaris Moore provided timely support through her meticulous proofreading of the completed text.

This book did not come into its final form without the kind and supportive guidance and feedback of Shambhala's able editors: first and foremost, Kendra Crossen Burroughs, who was a strong proponent of its value for spiritual seekers, and later, Liz Shaw, who nursed it through to completion. I am indebted to both my editors and Shambhala for making it possible for *The Unfolding Now* to find its way to you.

THE UNFOLDING
NOW

CHAPTER I

Loving the Real

WITHOUT HEART, WE ARE not really human. And the possibility of having an authentic and deeply satisfying human life is only a pipe dream when our love is not directed to what truly fulfills the heart. To find true fulfillment, many of us at some point in life turn to the spiritual search. But what is it in spirituality that gives this fulfillment? Where does this deep satisfaction come from?

To answer this question, we need to find out why we become involved in the spiritual search in the first place. What are we looking for when we begin the journey? To experience new and remarkable states of consciousness? To travel to extraordinary realms beyond our everyday world? To be liberated from the difficulties and constraints of the world? Or are we looking to enrich and deepen the meaning of the lives we are living here on Earth? If our aim is to engage in our spiritual work so that it can impact and transform the way we live, we have to begin by seeing what we are actually doing in our lives. What are we up to? What do we really want?

We live in a big, noisy, distracting world. And when we look deeply into our hearts most of us find that one of the primary things we want is something quite simple: We want peace. We want rest, ease, and quiet. We want to stop our constant doing. We want space from all the struggle, conflict, desire, fear, and hatred. We are drawn to people who are peaceful, to situations where we can have peace and quiet. Simplicity without stress. Being at ease. In some very deep sense, this desire leads to greater fulfillment than our urges for pleasure, happiness, and freedom, for without this ease of simply being, none of the other things we pursue will truly satisfy us.

Most of us tend to look for quiet by changing our physical surroundings. We look outside of ourselves for this peace and ease of being. But much of the constant activity is actually inside our head. Even if we go away from the highways, from the supermarkets, from the TVs and telephones to sit and meditate—even in the quiet of our own room—it doesn't mean that we are getting away from the noise inside. And why is there so much noise, so much activity? The answer, of course, comes to us as more noise—more activity in our mind. To explain, analyze, work with, or discuss why our minds are so busy can only increase the busyness inside. You have probably already noticed that yourself.

So our mind tends to be noisy and busy, just like the world we live in. We are hearing so much noise, that after a while we don't know what we are doing here. There isn't enough quiet space to feel ourselves in a simple, immediate way; we don't have enough space to just be ourselves. All this extra stuff is competing for our attention. And if we do make the space to feel ourselves, what we find inside is mostly busyness, so the possibility of peace seems like a pipe dream. That is how our world is, how our life is, and how our mind is, too. Most of the time, we don't even question it; we think that is just how it is. It is a noisy world, so we learn to live with it.

No wonder that for some people, getting ready to leave this world is what it takes to quiet down. If the dying process is slow, by the time they finally leave, it has usually quieted down inside. You might have seen this in someone you know. Often it requires something that radical for us to be quiet, something like death. In this book, we want to learn how to let death quiet us while we live—

how to be quiet in the midst of the noise before we reach the end of life.

So much is going on in the world and in our minds that it reminds me of being in a movie theater nowadays. You go there to relax and enjoy a film, and more often than not, you are assaulted by loud noises. You can't even feel anything about what you are watching because of all the clanging and explosions, all the yelling and screaming, all the loud action and intense suspense. It is like entering a war zone. Everything is turned up to the maximum.

Living in our minds is actually like that. Have you noticed how busy your mind is just reading these words? The mind is always occupied with reactions, judgments, questions, associations, desires, and attitudes. And we have become like teenagers who are used to all that noise. We think the noise is what reality is and no longer recognize what is truly real. We are not feeling ourselves in that intimate, simple, relaxed way that we like but may have forgotten exists—the feeling we would like to have when we go to a movie to relax and watch something interesting.

In contrast to our modern multiplex cinemas with their Hollywood blockbusters, what many of us would love is to go to an old-time movie theater where the sound is rather tame and quiet and the story evolves slowly, so we can actually follow what we feel about it. And we would love to be able to do the same thing with ourselves in our own experience, to be with ourselves in such a way that we can see where we are, notice what is happening, and know how we feel about it. This would let us feel more real.

What we miss when we don't feel that kind of simple quiet is an awareness of ourselves in our experience in its immediacy, in its fullness. Instead, we are hearing echoes, reverberations, and reflections. All of our ideals, our ideas, our projects, our worries, and our fears become noise that overwhelms our immediate experience and the subtle sense of what we are. The preciousness of just simply being here in the moment is forgotten, lost in the shuffle, lost in the noise.

The spiritual journey is not about having experiences, interesting insights, or unusual perceptions, although those will often arise as part of it. I am not saying they don't have their place and value, but they are not the point of the inner journey. Inner practice is basically a matter of settling and quieting. It is about settling into the simplicity of just being ourselves and feeling our realness—being in reality instead of in the echoes of reality.

THE NATURE OF BEING REAL

Reality is not what is usually reflected in our minds. Reality is so much cleaner and simpler, and in comparison to the noisy world of our usual inner experience, so much more settled and at ease. There is an exquisite intimacy in us just feeling ourselves, being ourselves. And when we are quiet and settled like that, we simply feel real. We recognize the realness of our Being, the realness of our awareness.

Being real happens when the noise has subsided and the complexities dissolve and we are experiencing ourselves just as we are in our true condition. Not the reflection, not the picture, not the echo, not the memory, not the thought, not the reaction, but the thing itself. Usually, we assume that reality is full of all kinds of sounds and noise, and we believe most of what we hear. We focus on what the noise is saying or else we are busy responding to it—defending, justifying, reacting, explaining, judging, thinking, planning, remembering. But those activities are just the reflections of what is real.

Being real is what we are, what we truly are, and we experience it in the moment. And being real doesn't require that we experience anything in particular. It is more about the *way* we are being, rather than *what* we are being. It is like the difference between hearing one thousand loud noises and hearing one single note, simple and gentle, which makes us feel closer to who and what we are. Closer to our heart. At that moment, we feel that our heart is alive and tender. Our heart has its tenderness when we are feeling ourselves. We recognize ourselves in that tenderness, in that nearness to what is real.

When we have lived through years of noise and drama, pushes and pulls, manipulation and struggle, and maybe after many years of spiritual practice or work, it is possible to recognize that what is needed is to simply be real. We want to be what is real in us, to remember or recognize the realness of what it is to be a human being—an aware, awake being—and then experience this beingness consciously. In other words, what we are is about reality, about being real—not about getting anywhere in particular but simply to be as we are. We want to learn how we can be here in as real a way as possible: How can I be completely here and completely myself, or as completely as possible? How can my atoms, which are scattered, vibrating, and oscillating in some kind of frenzy, slow down, collect, and settle here as what I am?

THE DESIRE FOR BEING REAL

As we go along, you will see that we can learn to be real, to connect with and become aware of our realness. And you will notice that something about this attracts us. We are attracted to the condition of being real. We like being real. And this is because we know the difference between being real and so much of what our usual experience is. Most of these things are not what is real; they are just reflections and distortions.

Many people get caught up in spiritual experiences and perceptions and all kinds of interesting, subtle impressions, some of which can be exciting and uplifting. But there is nothing like the simplicity of being oneself—settling into yourself, just being there, recognizing what you are, and feeling the sense of intimacy and realness of that. All of the inner journey, all of spiritual practice, ultimately comes down to this: that we are able to be genuinely what we are. If you want to do inner practice in order to develop certain powers or go to other dimensions or have special experiences, you still don't know what spiritual work is. And this is because you are not yet recognizing what reality is or what being real means.

On the other hand, you already appreciate being real if you genuinely want to do inner work for its own sake. Being real means being the way you are when you are by yourself and quiet: "I know this is me and I know what that is like and I am comfortable being it. I have no conflict about it. And when I am interacting with someone, it is that reality of who I am that is interacting." People don't generally make the effort to do inner work if they don't want to be real, if they don't feel that being real is something good, something they want, something they appreciate. There is something precious about being real in an interaction, something that cannot be analyzed. Being real has nothing to do with getting something or giving something, being seen or making the other feel seen—none of that. It is just me, as what I am, actually being the one who is doing or saying something.

But it would be missing the point to want to be real so that we will feel satisfied or happy or accomplished. No, we want to be real because in fact we love being real. We love reality and we love to feel it, to see it, and to be it as much as possible. Only when we can slow down and rest in the simple, precious moments of living, can we recognize that we love this quality of realness for its own sake and not because of what it does for us.

We don't love it because it makes us feel good or is good for us, or because it means an attainment of one kind or another, or because it represents some kind of enlightenment or advancement. We love it because we know that when we are real, we are home—no matter the sensation or the flavor. Sometimes being real means allowing pain or accepting a painful truth. Yet something in us aligns with an inner ground of authenticity when we are real. We love it because of its inherent rightness in our soul, the sense of "Aha, here I am and there is nothing to do but be."

THE LOVE OF BEING REAL

Wanting to be real indicates having a measure of self-love, some kind of love of what we are. So when we want to move toward being real, we are already expressing a lovingness and an appreciation that is essential to spiritual work. If that lovingness is not there, our practice is done for the wrong reason; it is part of the noise. What I'm pointing to is not a selfish kind of self-love; it is not possessiveness or self-centeredness. This heart attitude toward realness—this feeling that our consciousness, our soul, our awareness, has about being real—is very subtle and difficult to explain. To recognize this appreciation for the real in ourselves indicates that we have already developed a certain level of maturity and a specific guidance for our practice.

It is a precious moment when we recognize this love, this appreciation—when we know that we are not practicing to accomplish something. I am not meditating, praying, chanting, or working on myself to make myself better. I am not doing this work so that I will be as good as the next person or because I have an idea or some ideal I developed or heard about and decided was a good thing to go after. It is not a matter of going after anything. It is just a matter of settling down with myself.

It means learning how to recognize our agitated activity, our noise, and how not to go along with it. Instead we learn to simply settle, relax, and be. And I don't mean that when you relax and be, you just sit and meditate. Meditation is something we practice, but ultimately, engaging inner practice and living life are not two things. Being real, learning to be real, is our practice in every moment; it becomes the living of our real life. And being real transcends any dimension, any experience, any perception—regardless of the content. It is just the experience of feeling no distance from yourself— no dissociation, no scattering, no dispersion, no distraction. And the more you recognize this collectedness, this presence, this hereness, this settledness, the more you have a sense of being real, of reality.

So at some point, we see that spiritual practice is a matter of learning reality, learning to recognize realness, learning to be real, and learning to be ourselves in our realness. And we see that we are only interested in learning these things if we have the appreciation and love of being real. We have to love being genuine to go through the trouble and the discipline of inner work. It is because we are being authentic, because we are approaching reality, because we are being touched by reality, that we love it and are willing to go through the various processes of acknowledging and seeing the truth— whether painful or scary or pleasurable.

Our first step is to recognize the love and appreciation in us that draws us to reality. Regardless of what motivation we start with for doing inner work, our love of reality at some point reveals itself if we are sincere. We recognize that we just like being near reality, we love being comfortable with it and having no conflicts about it, and we like being as intimate with it as possible. We want to become so intimate that we simply are what is real . . . and that is what we love.

EXPLORATION SESSION

Your Relationship to Being Real

This exploration will help you clarify your own relationship to reality and realness and how it affects your life and your spiritual journey.

When have you felt most real in your life and how did you recognize it? Think of a situation in which you felt you were truly being yourself, perhaps when it was a real challenge to do so. What responses did you notice in your mind? In your heart? In your body? Contrast this with another incident when you felt distant from your own realness or authenticity. What did you experience then?

Do you believe it is a good or moral thing to be real? Is being real part of your spiritual ideal? Does the desire to be real play a part in your interest in this book?

Is realness something you want more of in your life? If so, why? What would you give up in order to be more real? Do you feel compelled toward being authentically yourself? Do you love it? If so, has the love of realness motivated your choices or led you to practice in certain ways in your life?

CHAPTER 2

Learning to Be Real

L EARNING TO BE REAL IS a full-time job. It doesn't work to just practice it at certain times. But to make that kind of commitment, you have to love and appreciate reality. You have to *want* to be real at any cost. You have to *love* being real—even if you don't like what you're feeling or who you think you are in any particular moment. That kind of love is the most powerful motive—the real inspiration—for our inner work. If your longing for reality is lukewarm or if it comes and goes, where will the passion and inner support come from to sustain yourself as you learn to be real? The more you are in touch with your love of being real, the more you will be inspired . . . and the more you will be fired up to do the work.

But what does it mean to be real?

BEING YOURSELF

You can't be real if you are not yourself. You cannot be something other than what you are and be real. Observe and you will discover that most of the time, you are not real because you are not yourself.

So what are you then? Who are you being? What are you doing? Most of us are being and acting out an image of ourselves—an idea, a picture, a concept. If, in this moment, you are an image of who you truly are, you can only be distant from yourself.

And most of us are even further away from our real self than that, because we are an image of something *other* than what we are—for example, an image of our body or an image of how we were as a child. And the unrealness becomes greater still when we are being an image or picture of someone else altogether, such as of one of our parents.

So what is the practice of being real? It is the same as the practice of being oneself. To be real means, "I am not an idea of myself. I am not pretending to be myself. I am not being in reaction to something or someone or their image of me. I am being what I actually am." But it is not as though one can just stop being unreal and start being oneself. After all, who knows what that actually means? How are you going to try to be yourself? It is not as though you have many selves on a shelf, and you can take the real one down and put it on.

The good news is that no matter how distant you are from yourself, something in your experience in any given moment expresses who you really are. You can wander far from your realness—you can even become disconnected from it—but who is it that is far away or is disconnected? It's still you. Whatever your experience, wherever you are, whatever you are perceiving, is connected to what and who you really are.

If you reflect a bit, you will notice that you are always experiencing something. There is always an impression, always an awareness, of something happening in the moment. Right now, a number of things are happening, and you are aware of them. As you are reading this sentence, for example, you are seeing, comprehending, and perhaps also thinking, feeling, sensing the pressure of your body on a chair, or hearing sounds around you.

So we are always someplace in the experiential field. That place is always changing, but we are always someplace in the field of myriad possibilities. There's nothing esoteric in that; it is merely what we are experiencing every moment. You can recognize from your own life that the only time you are not experiencing anything is when you are in deep, dreamless sleep. So the moment there is consciousness, there is experience. This applies whether the experience is special (according to your value system) or quite ordinary. Think about what's going on while you're having breakfast. You are moving your arms, you are chewing, you are experiencing tastes and flavors in your mouth and movement and textures in your hand, and perhaps you are having a sense of appreciation or revulsion or boredom. Thoughts, feelings, imaginings—all of these are happening.

So, something is always going on! And whatever that something is, is related to who you are in the sense that it is more reflective of who *you* are than of who someone else is. If you are sitting in meditation, your experience is more a reflection of who you are than a reflection of who President Bush is, for instance. So if you are going to find yourself, you don't go look into George Bush's experience, you go look into your own experience.

TRUE NATURE

What does this fact mean for our practice? To learn to be ourselves, we have to start with what we have—and what we always have is our experience in the moment. If we allow ourselves to be in our experience in the moment—to feel it, to see it, to taste it, to hear it, to smell it, to be aware of it—it becomes possible for us to find out what we are and to be who we are.

To be ourselves, or to be real, basically means that we are being our true self, or we are being the realness of who we are. You may have heard it said, "My True Nature means the true or the self-existing nature of who I am." That can sound esoteric, but it just means that your True Nature is not false, not fabricated, not created by anybody; it is what you truly are. It is the real you.

Being *who* we are requires first finding out *where* we are. And although being aware of where we are does not necessarily mean we are being ourselves yet, it's a start. That's because it contains an element or flavor of our true self. And that flavor, or that element, is what we call "truth." So wherever we are, whatever our experience happens to be, is related to our True Nature in some way. It may be distant or disconnected, or it may be a reaction, a reflection, or a substitute. But it still is somehow related to who we truly are.

In the early stages of our practice, we often don't know what this relationship is. But we can begin by looking at our experience and finding where we are: I am sitting here, bored . . . or, I'm hungry and impatient as I am driving around trying to find a restaurant that's open . . . or, I am lying in bed feeling guilty about what I just said to my husband . . . or, I am sitting in front of my computer, fidgety, worried about my stocks . . . or, I am trying to relax and I can't stop thinking . . . or, I am meditating and I am feeling empty and anxious. Looking closely, you discover that each one of these is somehow related to who you truly are.

The key is: If you can find a way to understand how your present experience is related to your True Nature, then you are closer to accessing that True Nature—and that access is called *truth*. So how can you do that? At first, even when you have some sense about where you are, you don't understand all that is happening in a given situation. Most of our experience is half conscious and not comprehended. When you are more fully intimate with your experience and have some real understanding of it, you then can say that you are seeing the truth of your experience. But what is the truth of our experience, and why is there such a thing?

Truth is always an expression of our True Nature, which is the ultimate truth. To understand your experience, you need to see how it is related to your True Nature, how it is connected to who and what you really are. That is why every time you understand your experience and see the truth, you feel a little more real, you feel nearer to your True Nature—because you are beginning to see how the experience is related to who you really are.

Let's say I am spending time doing a hobby I usually enjoy. After a while, I recognize that I am feeling bored. If I attempt to dispel my boredom, I will be resisting where I am. Because I want to be more real, I choose to stay with my experience even if it is unpleasant. (We will see more about this as we go along.) When I explore my boredom, I realize I'm bored because I am feeling a kind of emptiness, a kind of meaninglessness. I am seeing the truth of my experience, which is the reality of my feeling boredom, which I experience as a meaningless emptiness. I see the truth and that makes me feel a little more real. But I don't yet understand in my mind how it is related to my True Nature.

But if I think about it a little bit, I can see that where I am and how I am feeling are connected to my True Nature. The fact that I am feeling a meaningless emptiness reflects the fact that I have a True Nature and that I am distant from it. This is because True Nature has implicit in it a sense of significance. If I had no True Nature, there would be no way to feel a meaningless emptiness. Why is that? Usually, I take meaninglessness to indicate a loss of some external source of meaning that I have been accustomed to. However, if I pay attention to the experience of meaninglessness itself, I can recognize that it actually feels like a loss of contact with my own sense of significance. In other words, I implicitly know what meaning feels like in my soul and that feeling is missing.

So as we inquire into *where* we are, experience the truth, and follow the thread of truth, that thread eventually will connect us with the truth of *what* we are. That is why truth brings more reality. Truth and reality are related; they are two sides of the same thing. The more we see the truth of where we are in the moment, the more we recognize something about the relationship between *where* we are and *what* we are. That recognition makes the distance between them shorter, and we feel more real. And that is why when we are real, we tend to see more of the truth of the situation; it works both ways.

BEING AWARE OF WHERE YOU ARE

If we are interested in being real, we naturally become interested in being as clear as possible about what is happening, and we want to experience it as intimately and fully as possible—we want to be totally in touch with it. If I am feeling anxiety, for instance, or fear, or terror, I am aware of it. Well, what does that mean? I don't mean looking at it from far away through a telescope: "Oh, there is fear over there." No, it's about *feeling* what the terror is like, what the anxiety is like, what the anger is like, what the love is like, what the pain in my knee is like.

Being aware means immediacy. It means that the tentacles of my soul are wrapping themselves around the feeling, penetrating it and all its parts, feeling it from inside and outside—because my awareness extends everywhere. If I am not fully aware of the situation, how am I going to find out the truth about it? And if I am not interested in paying attention to what is happening now, what does it mean when I say that I love being myself?

When you love somebody, you want to find out everything about them, don't you? When you love something, what do you want to do with it? You want to know it. Love always translates into awareness, into knowing. If you love somebody, you want to see them, you want to know them, you want to be as completely familiar with them as possible. If you are really interested in being yourself, that interest begins with the awareness of where you are at this very moment. Being *who* you are can only arise from the love of being *where* you are.

It now becomes clear that being where you are is central to the practice of being real. And this is not separate from the practice of self-inquiry, for it is self-inquiry that will ultimately allow us to simply be by bringing us into more intimate contact with what we are being. Self-inquiry consists of two basic elements:

1. Observing your experience until you become clear about where you are. That is, becoming aware at any moment of what you are actually experiencing. Just remember: Since you are always someplace, it is always possible to recognize where you are.

2. Beginning to ask, "What is making this happen?" The moment you ask this question, the inquiry begins to expand our experience of where we are. Since you are not able to immediately comprehend most of your experience, it is natural that you will want to know,

"What is making me feel this way?" in any given situation. As you ask what is happening, as you become interested in understanding more about where you are, you will begin to see some truth about your experience. And that understanding will eventually lead you to grasp the relationship between your True Nature and where you are.

Seeing something that we call truth—something that gives meaning or coherence to what is happening—gives us an overall picture we can comprehend. It's not only a mental explanation but a felt sense of it being experientially meaningful to us. It makes sense to our heart, to our soul. As this meaning is revealed, we have the experience of insight in our heart, we discover some truth, something we can then know in our mind. And if we continue being where we are and exploring from where we are, the discovery of the truth becomes a process, a deepening thread.

THE LIGHT OF TRUE NATURE

The recognition of the truth—if you truly glimpse it, if you see it in its actuality—brings more awareness, which opens up your experience. It means that you can see more—as if there were more light available. This is referred to as the light of awareness. It is the penetration of the light of your True Nature into your experience. When you see the truth, when you have insight about what is happening, it is as though a light had broken through. That is what it means to have insight: insight brings enlightenment. And it is actually more literal than that. You see ignorance and shadow clearing away and brightness coming through into your experience. What is the light that does this? It is the light of your nature. It is the light of who and what you are. So, by seeing the truth of where you are, you are learning to be real and you are learning to be yourself.

Let's take my earlier example: "I'm bored because I am experiencing some kind of meaningless emptiness." If I explore why I'm feeling meaningless and empty, I recognize that it is because I am identifying with a representation, a particular image. When I explore why that makes me feel empty and meaningless, I recognize that this identification disconnects me from simply being, and when I am not just simply being here, I am not being myself.

What I have just explained sounds simple. But I remember spending ten days or ten weekends in the past explaining it. It is actually a giant step to understand this. So let's break down what we're trying to understand into these three smaller pieces that are easier to digest:

1. What is our practice?
2. What are the insights that underlie our practice?
3. How is awareness necessary for our practice to begin and how does our awareness develop?

The answer to the first question is simple: The practice is learning to be real, which requires understanding what it means to be ourselves.

Second, the basic insights that underlie our practice are:

- We learn to be ourselves by recognizing the truth of our experience.
- We cannot recognize the truth of our experience if we don't know where we are in the moment.
- We won't recognize where we are if we resist being where we are. Not allowing ourselves to be where we are prevents us from understanding our experience for what it is, and we won't see the truth of the situation.
- When we don't see the truth of the situation, it is because something is obstructing the shaft of light that could be breaking through.

Practically speaking, what this comes down to is that we need to be able to see where we are. Now *where* we are is not *what* we are—at least at the beginning of the path. What we are is our True Self, our True Nature. But we have already seen that by understanding where we are right now, we can recognize our distance from our True Nature.

But how can we see where we are if we don't attend to the moment, if we don't pay attention to what is happening? We need to be interested in what is happening, we need to be aware of what is arising in our experience. The points below will help clarify this third key element of practice.

What the practice is: Bringing awareness to the present moment, every moment, moment by moment.

What it means: Simply paying attention to what is going on, being aware of what is happening.

What to do: Attend to whatever is happening at this very moment. You only need to be aware of the facts of your experience, whatever they may be: I'm talking . . . I'm sitting . . . My back is sore . . . I'm breathing . . . I'm hungry . . . I'm bored . . . The food I'm eating is tasteless . . .

Why it's needed: If we really love being real, that love will have to translate into an interest in what is going on now. We can't *be* where we are if we don't *see* where we are.

What it can look like in real life: If I am bored, but I don't know that I am bored, how will I ever know that meaninglessness underlies my boredom? If I am bored, but I think it's just because the food I'm eating is tasteless, there is no chance to understand the situation. So the first thing I need to do is to attend to what is happening. Maybe the first thing that strikes me is not that I am bored, but that the food is tasteless. Maybe I am bored, but I don't feel I am bored. Instead, I feel it's me rather than the food that is tasteless. Or perhaps I am not paying attention to the fact that the food is tasteless because I'm on the phone talking to somebody because I don't want to taste the tastelessness. And the food is tasteless because I am actually bored. And I am actually bored because life feels meaningless to me. And because I prefer not being aware of any of that, I end up talking on the phone about a movie or some family business.

How it works: As we become aware, we begin to recognize how we were *not* aware. The more we are aware of the situation, the more we recognize how we don't understand it, how there are gaps in it, how it doesn't make sense. That gives us the opportunity to inquire, become more aware, and find the truth in the situation.

What can get in the way: First, most of us will want to pay attention to our moment-to-moment experience only if it is pleasant—if the food tastes good and we're happy, or if we feel secure and loved. Then maybe we'll pay a little attention, maybe we will be present enough to experience how the food tastes. But most of the time, we are too scattered to do that.

Second, it's easy to fall into the trap of wanting something from your experience or wanting something to happen. True awareness means simply perceiving what actually is happening, and recognizing that it has value in and of itself, that it is something we can appreciate.

What must come first: Our appreciation and love of reality must become our primary interest. Not interest in the sense of attachment—wanting something from it—but interest in the sense of wanting to know it, wanting to be aware of it, wanting to feel it, to experience it as fully as possible, to be as intimate with it as we can. If your love for being real is strong, you are naturally interested and inspired to be aware.

What we're really after: Understanding any situation is a matter of having greater and greater awareness of what is happening. The more aware we are of what is happening, the more that awareness becomes dynamic and reveals the meaning of what is going on. That awareness gives a coherent sense to our experience, which makes us feel more real, more genuine, because it brings us closer to what we are.

Sometimes when you are aware, you may feel that you're efforting to be aware and sometimes you feel like it's just happening. Either way, it doesn't matter for your practice. The fact is, awareness is always happening on its own. When it feels as though we are doing something in order to be aware, it means that we are disciplining our awareness by attending to the situation and thus counteracting our tendency to distract ourselves. Because in general, we tend to resist being aware. So, when we feel in some sense that *we* are doing it, we are using will or discipline. But when you investigate that closely, you will see it is a doing that is an undoing of our resistance to awareness.

You want to practice awareness as much as possible. What you need to remember about your practice is that at all times—whether sitting in meditation or having a meal or talking with a friend or listening to somebody giving a lecture—you can be present and aware. You can remember to be present to what is going on. Learning to be real must begin with recognizing what is real in our experience, and that always begins with being aware of where we are in the present moment.

EXPLORATION SESSION

Bringing Awareness to Where You Are

This exercise will help you to attend more fully to where you are. Begin with your experience right now. What is going on? Where are you in this moment? What is happening to you? What are you feeling, sensing, thinking, noticing around you?

You want to feel where you are. You want to see it, experience it, recognize it, understand it. You don't want to go anywhere; you are not trying to accomplish anything. You just want to find out where you happen to be in this moment and to explore where you are consciously, fully and with awareness and presence.

After you've done this for a while, consider the experience you've just had. Your awareness can expand and deepen, or become limited and more constricted. What expanded your awareness? What limited it?

CHAPTER 3

Hands Off Your
Experience

In CHAPTER 2, WE DISCOVERED that the way we learn how to be real, how to be ourselves, is by knowing our True Nature. To be real and to be ourselves means being our True Nature. And to be just where we are is the closest thing in ordinary experience to being our True Nature.

It is useful to note here that the teaching about being where we are is not necessarily the most profound teaching, nor is it necessarily the teaching that will immediately bring us into the deepest condition or state of consciousness. But it is a teaching that is appropriate for any condition—for each of us, wherever we are.

All the instructions on being real actually come from True Nature. So, the challenge is to learn how to listen and find out what our True Nature is telling us about being real and how to practice.

TRUE NATURE SAYS,
"HANDS OFF!"

Our minds usually want to make things complicated, but the basic instruction of True Nature is quite simple. It says: "Hands off!" That is the primary teaching. Don't do anything. Completely cease anything you are trying to do to yourself. Hands off your own experience.

People naturally wonder what that means, because "hands off" sounds like passivity, that we should just let everything happen to us and not take any action in the world. But True Nature doesn't mean hands off the activities of your life; it means hands off your experience. However you experience yourself, whatever arises in your awareness—that is to be left alone. That is not to say that when you are hungry, you shouldn't eat. And it isn't to suggest that if somebody is attacking you, you shouldn't defend yourself.

I'll give you a simple example. Let's say you take a bite of a peach and discover that it is rotten. What is the teaching? Hands off! Hands off means that I take a bite, I experience the rotten taste, so I put the peach down, but I don't put away my experience of the rotten taste. Many people misunderstand hands off, thinking it means that they should continue eating the peach. But that's not what it means. The rotten taste is already in my mouth. I already have it as an inner sensation that is arising in my experience. If I try to put that sensation away, I am dividing myself; I am saying no to something in my experience. So when we say, "hands off," we mean hands off whatever arises in our inner experience.

Hands off also applies when the peach tastes wonderful. When we taste how good it is, we sometimes want to hold on to that experience. Then hands off means that I eat the peach, and I enjoy it without trying to intensify the experience or make it last longer. It does not mean that you make yourself stop eating the peach so you can practice nonattachment. The trick to hands off is that you enjoy the delicious peach as it is—without trying to hold on to it, without putting away your feelings, and without having to put away the peach.

In the case of the rotten peach, you taste it and you put it away; with the delicious peach, you taste it and continue eating it—but in both instances, your mind is not doing anything to manipulate your inner experience.

That is what True Nature teaches us. It doesn't do anything to itself. It just is. So what we need to learn is how to be just like that. That is what the practice is. True Nature doesn't say, "Do this or do that." Rather, it tells us *not* to do things that interfere: "No pushing, don't manipulate, that's not it." Whenever we want to do something to ourselves, it tells us, "No, hands off—leave your experience alone."

So, to practice is to learn how to leave yourself alone. Imagine you are with a person or a group of people that is always telling you what to do: "Do this . . . this is no good . . . you should change that . . . no, no, this is terrible; do it the other way." How would you feel? You would want to be free of them, right? We naturally dislike coercion when it comes to our inner experience. Even if you don't have people like that in your life, the problem is that those people are all inside of you. Their voices keep trying to push you in one direction or another.

And if we have been doing inner practice, one of the more prominent voices is always trying to make us better, more spiritual. We are trying to make ourselves enlightened. We are trying to squeeze ourselves into some kind of state. We are trying to corral ourselves into a particular condition. So, let's say you sit down to meditate one morning. If you are sitting because you want to do something to yourself to get someplace, then you are interfering. If you just sit—that's all—without doing anything, you are practicing. But that's rarely the case. That's because there are such things as spiritual schools and teachings and practices, so the moment we sit to meditate, we think we are going to do something to get someplace.

That is the trap, the paradox, of spiritual practice. You are trying to learn not to do anything, but the very fact that you are sitting implies that you are striving to accomplish something, to reach some kind of spiritual state, or maybe attain an enlightened condition. The moment we go in with that attitude, we are already pushing in our consciousness, in our soul; we are trying to make things go in a certain direction. An operation has been set in motion to achieve a certain result.

So even though our spiritual teachings tell us that there is nothing to accomplish, that isn't real for us, so we keep manipulating our experience. We can't help but feel that we need to accomplish being ourselves in some way. Now there is nothing new about that self-manipulation; even before we learned anything about spiritual work, we were always trying to change our everyday experience. We judged it and devalued it and tweaked it and squeezed it. We pushed it and pulled it and held on to it. We have always tried to make ourselves feel something that is different from how we actually feel, because we have it in our minds that however things are in our experience is not the way they should be.

For instance, maybe when you were growing up, you were never able to accomplish small things such as being patient with your little sister or brother or always being good to please your mother. Now the stakes are higher, so you are really in a fix. Now you are not just trying to be good or patient, you are going for enlightenment! Now your job is to figure out how you can manage to get enlightened, so you focus on doing spiritual practices—chanting and meditating and inquiry and whirling or whatever it is you do—and you never leave yourself alone.

But what practice does our True Nature recommend?

We can be guided here by noticing the way that True Nature relates to whatever is happening to us. Let's say you are feeling pain or fear or happiness. Or maybe you are feeling divided or guilty or scared or full of longing. What does your True Nature do? It doesn't do anything. It is simply aware of whatever you are feeling; it is interested, empathic, attuned to what is happening. It wants to experience the feeling fully, be there for it with kindness, gentleness. True Nature doesn't try to push. It doesn't *try* to do anything, and it doesn't *do* anything—it just is. And in its is-ness, the necessary qualities emerge. If compassion is needed, compassion emerges. If love is needed, love emerges. If strength is needed, strength emerges. True Nature doesn't lift a finger.

TRUE NATURE IS AWARE
AND ATTUNED

True Nature does nothing, but it is naturally aware because it is pure awareness. If we just let things be—if we don't control them or try to direct them—we are naturally, simply aware. And in this awareness, we are present to whatever is happening. True Nature is so loving, so kind—infinite in its kindness and compassion and intelligence—that it relates to each condition exactly according to what that condition needs. And it doesn't give you an instruction that you cannot relate to. It doesn't try to tell you to practice something you cannot practice. In our work, we discover that True Nature responds to our limitations—our stuckness, our lack of development, our reactivity—appropriately and with attunement and kindness.

So that is what our practice is. We are learning how True Nature would approach our situation in the moment—how it would hold it, how it would relate to it. And we especially want to know this when we are reactive or scared or feeling stuck. That's when it's especially hard to know how to just be in a natural condition. You might hear people say, "Just be in your True Nature; remember what it is to be yourself and just be that." For some people, that might work, but most people can't do that at any time, much less when things are difficult.

We never need to take the position that we have to pull or push ourselves into the complete purity or nonduality of our True Nature. That would be like trying to push a camel through the eye of a needle, as some spiritual traditions express it. True Nature is compassionate and appropriate, so the first thing it does is to help the camel walk. It doesn't try to push the camel anywhere, much less through the needle's eye.

TRUE NATURE HAS
NO PREFERENCES

The way True Nature approaches all questions is by being open with full awareness and understanding of the particular reality that a person is operating in. For example, if a person embraces reality as non-dual, as having no separating boundaries, True Nature is very open to that and will respond accordingly. Whatever beliefs, assumptions, and limitations a person has, True Nature is open to see those without trying to change them. If an experience is limited, True Nature sees it in its limitation and doesn't try to make it be different. True Nature really has no preferences.

So, one thing we can learn from True Nature is to have no preference, no choice; we don't need to choose what to experience. Our experience always simply happens. If we try to choose and say, "This is good, this is bad, this situation should include this and not that," we are already separating ourselves from True Nature; we are already not practicing.

True Nature shows us that to be where we are means having an awareness that embraces whatever is—whatever our perceptions are, at whatever level, in whatever condition or state we are in. That awareness embraces our experience completely, with immediate feeling, with as much understanding as possible. The awareness contacts the experience, holds it, embraces it—just by being there, by being with it, in it, around it.

And when I say "being with it," I don't mean that the awareness is necessarily being with something separate from itself. For example, if I say that I am being with my hand now, does this mean that there have to be two things—me and my hand? I can be with my hand and yet my hand is mine, it is part of me. It is the same with your thoughts. You can be with your thoughts and see that they are separate from you, or you can be with them and see that they are not separate from you. Either way is valid; what's important is that you see whatever it is you are experiencing.

TRUE NATURE MEANS
NONDOING AND SURRENDER

To be where we are really is a form of surrender to whatever is happening. And that surrender is an awareness that embraces whatever our experience is. If I am feeling something and I see that I don't like it, then I embrace that I am feeling something *and* I embrace the fact that I don't like it. I don't take the position that I shouldn't have a negative response to what I am feeling.

This implies a certain trust and confidence in our nature. Usually we don't have that trust, so we want to take things into our own hands and twist them and turn them the way we want them to be. True Nature shows us that we have another option, which is to align with it in allowing our experience to be what it is.

So you can see from everything that has been said thus far that True Nature really doesn't do anything. It doesn't push and it doesn't hold on to anything. It simply relaxes, effortlessly, and is present with full awareness, embracing the immediacy of feeling and sensing our experience. That is the sense in which surrender is meant. It's not that we are going to do something: "Okay, now I am going to surrender." What are you going to do to surrender? I have never seen anybody surrendering. Nobody ever surrenders. Surrender means basically nondoing. It means not doing anything to what is arising in our experience. It means leaving ourselves and our experience alone.

When we have been pushing and pulling and resisting and controlling and then at some point we stop doing that, the transition can sometimes seem like surrender. When we have been holding ourselves together or remaining involved in an active, rigid mental process, and we recognize that and stop doing it, we call it surrender. But *stopping* doing something is not *doing* something. So, surrender is not an activity. And it is definitely not control.

To be where we are means that we leave our experience alone. We don't interfere with it, we don't say no to it, we don't try to grasp it. We don't say anything about it at all—no comment! Instead, we behold it, embrace it, be with it. And this absence of control, this effortless lack of manipulation, this hands off, can continue moment to moment, but the awareness of not doing anything will elude us if we are not carefully attending to what is happening. For instance, you may say, "I had an experience and I really surrendered. I was just there; I wasn't doing anything," and then the next moment say, "I think it was a wonderful experience. I wish I could have it again." As soon as you think that way, you are already trying to squeeze your soul, tying it with a rope so that that experience doesn't get away from you.

Without careful attention, we will begin to manipulate without even knowing it. By the time we wake up to the situation, we have already tied ourselves up in knots. But even then, if we are aware, we can catch ourselves trying to hold on or trying to push away or trying to control. As soon as we feel the impulse to go after something, to orient ourselves one way or another, we recognize that and simply do not engage it. We cease and desist.

True Nature is always steadfast in its nonmanipulation, its noninterference. And it doesn't cheat. It always refrains from interfering. We learn that as well in our practice. We learn how not to interfere and to be steadfast in our noninterference. And because True Nature just is, it will simply unfold—manifesting and revealing whatever needs to be revealed to us.

TRUE NATURE EVEN RESPONDS
TO OUR MEDDLING

True Nature is a pure research scientist. What does a pure scientist do? He or she explores to find out the truth of a situation. Pure scientists know that as they explore something, they should not interfere with it, should not add to or subtract from it, should not manipulate it one way or another. They just want to know what they are studying as it is, in its bare, naked condition. They don't desire anything from it; they just want to behold it and discover the truth of what it is.

As we have seen, our meddling mind never acts in the way that a pure scientist does. But True Nature, in its infinite kindness, will respond impeccably according to our meddling. It will bring out whatever wisdom or quality or insight is needed in relation to whatever meddling we are doing. That is why True Nature has many qualities—because we engage in many kinds of meddling!

In our ordinary condition of never leaving ourselves alone, our manipulation happens on all levels, from gross to subtle. We can be trying to push ourselves through the eye of a needle by molding our experience in some highly manipulative way, or we can be engaging in a subtle form of holding on simply by remembering a condition that we enjoyed in the past and trying to shift our consciousness in that direction.

As we continue our study, we will learn more about the various ways that we interfere with our experience. But however we interfere, it is always true that because we don't have the infinite wisdom, intelligence, and awareness that True Nature has, we don't know what should happen next in our inner experience. Doing anything to make our moment-to-moment experience different from what it is means we believe we are God; we believe we know how things should be.

So you might think, "Now I am going to meditate so I can experience pure peace." But who said that pure peace should be the next thing you experience?

"And later I will get into primordial awareness." Who said that is what is supposed to happen to you?

Do you see the arrogance in this kind of thinking? Who is saying these things anyway? This is why in our work, we say, "I don't know what should come next in my experience; it is not in my hands." This is the humility needed for True Nature to move our experience to whatever condition it wants to bring about, which is usually the condition we specifically, personally, need at that moment. It might be primordial awareness, it might be peace—but it might be jealousy, or hunger, or even death. We don't know.

So whether we are meditating or doing inquiry exercises or having a meal or talking with a friend or doing our job, we can always practice by being present, by being aware of what is happening in our experience and not doing anything to it.

Because awareness is a manifestation of True Nature, it is natural for there to be awareness. But awareness is also necessary so we can recognize how we are meddling. We are usually meddling in a thousand different ways, but we often only notice one or two ways. Why? Because we are not completely aware of the situation. The more aware we are, the more we see the meddling, and the more we see the meddling, the better the possibility of ceasing and desisting, of not continuing to meddle.

Now if you catch yourself meddling, that doesn't mean you are doing something wrong. Let's establish that right away because for sure you are going to catch yourself doing just that. When you meditate or practice, for example, you will find yourself interfering, manipulating yourself, splitting yourself. Since we know this is going to happen, we practice with it. We see it, we let it be, and we don't do anything to it.

Remember that ceasing to meddle doesn't mean that you do something to stop. Just being aware that you are meddling—and seeing what meddling does—is usually sufficient for it to stop by itself. You won't have the feeling that *you* are stopping it; it just stops.

And if you don't do anything, you might begin to experience feelings arise in response to the meddling. You might feel kindness in response to the suffering involved in the meddling. You might feel the determination not to meddle, or you might feel the strength and the capacity to say, "I will be able to stay steadfast and not interfere." Or you might feel enough love just to be genuine and not divided in yourself.

EXPLORATION SESSION

Recognizing Your Own Meddling

Think of a challenging or uncomfortable incident or situation you went through recently. As you review it from the beginning, explore all the ways you tended to meddle with yourself while it was happening. How did you try to internally direct the experience—corral it, control it, change it, improve it, shape it?

Notice whether you meddle with yourself as you are recalling and writing about the situation. It is important to be as kind a researcher as possible so you don't judge yourself for what you find.

CHAPTER 4

Making Space
for Everything

You may have noticed that we are taking one little step at a time. To take even one step in our personal journey usually requires a lot of work and understanding. Much growing, maturing, and learning is involved, for instance, in going from seeing where you are to not meddling with where you are. And that includes working through many obstacles and patterns. However, in this book, we are not exploring the issues that arise with each of these topics. We are just looking at our practice of being real, exploring how things manifest in our practice, and discovering what guidance is available to support us as we take each step. Our desire, in whatever we are experiencing, is to be able to answer the question: How can I practice being real in relation to this experience that I am having right now?

As you are working with this book, be aware that you might notice all kinds of patterns and limitations in yourself coming up. For example, as you become more aware of the issues that make not meddling and not controlling your experience difficult, your tendencies and compulsions will become much more apparent. It is important to recognize this and allow the time and attention that is needed to address these issues. It is up to you to use your wisdom in finding the best way to attend to these personal conflicts and barriers.

TRUE NATURE AND NONINTERFERENCE

So let's take a deeper look at noninterference—keeping hands off—because it is one of the main keys to our practice. Noninterference is referred to in Chinese as *wu wei* (often translated "nonaction" or "nondoing"), and the followers of Kashmir Shaivism call it Anupaya Yoga. It is one of the tantric methods and, in that kind of yoga, it is usually reserved for the last stage of teaching. The instruction is this: Do not do anything to anything; just be present and aware, and whatever obstacle is there will dissolve to reveal its True Nature. If you feel an emotion completely, without adding anything to it, for example, it will transform to reveal its true condition, which is our True Nature in one particular flavor or another. Some emotions lead to joy, others to compassion or strength or peace—all distinct qualities of our True Nature.

But that direct transformation can happen only if we are already present and aware and fully in touch with our True Nature. Most of the time, however, we are not in that place. When we are in our usual consciousness, even if we can stay present with an emotion or manifestation, it doesn't immediately transform into its True Nature. It usually transforms into another emotion or feeling. In other words, we must undergo a several-step process before the experience finally reveals its True Nature.

Plus it has to be understood that an emotion is not just a simple reaction to whatever is happening in the present situation. Usually the emotion has an entire history. If you just let that emotion be, it begins to reveal that history and its implications. So, although True

Nature is always present, the infinitesimally thin barrier that separates emotional reality from True Nature may contain a hundred layers of history that are obscuring the truth. So, realization of True Nature is a gradual process.

INDIVISIBLE TRUE NATURE

We need to remember that the revelation of our True Nature is a process, so that we can be more realistic and more kind to ourselves about where we are. Thus our practice is to just be aware of and present with whatever is arising, to let it be and not do anything to it except allow our natural curiosity to unfold it and reveal what it is about. That process will at some point reveal the ultimate nature of that emotion.

As you notice, I didn't only say, "Be aware." I said, "Be aware and present." Awareness and presence are not two things, really, but if I only say, "Be aware," you might think of that in terms of normal awareness, that is, observing experience from a distance, with the detachment of a subject viewing an object. When I say, "aware and present," I am saying, "present to what you are aware of," which means that you are not only noticing it, but you are also in contact with it; you are touching it, feeling it, sensing its texture and quality. You are not only looking at it from the outside, you are aware of it from the inside as well and from all directions, from everywhere. So presence brings in the quality of *immediacy* of awareness, which means having no distance between the awareness and what we are aware of.

Presence gives a sense of immediacy, of fullness, of hereness in the experience. It gives a sense of immediacy and directness that suffuses the experience, that pervades it and fills it, so that our awareness, our consciousness, is not only observing it from a removed place but also from within it. It is as though our nerve endings were inside the experience, outside the experience, and in between; they are everywhere and feeling the experience in all its possibilities. That's when we really know the experience fully and completely. If we have that kind of awareness, then we recognize that to be aware of something is not just a function, and it is not just a capacity. The awareness, in fact, *is* our essential presence, our hereness, our substantiality.

This points to something important about our True Nature, our natural condition: True Nature is indivisible. True Nature cannot be divided; it doesn't have separate parts. It is not like a machine that has many parts, and it's not even like the body, which has many differentiated organs. Everything implicit in True Nature exists everywhere within it. It is not as though True Nature had love, for example, and this love is sitting in the gall bladder; it doesn't have a gall bladder. Love is everywhere in True Nature and so is awareness and so is strength. All of True Nature is one unified presence, and the same is true of awareness. True Nature and awareness are inseparable, and that fact can serve as guidance for our practice.

THE ONENESS OF OUR EXPERIENCE

Presence, like True Nature, is indivisible; it cannot be broken down into parts. It is unlimited, but not in the sense of being big, because presence has no size. It is unlimited in its qualities, possibilities, and potentiality. The reason this is important for our daily life is that when we are really being ourselves, we feel unified. We are whole—indivisible—there is no division, no contrariness within us; there are no parts opposing each other inside us.

Whatever impression, image, thought, feeling, sensation, or form of experience we become aware of always emerges within our consciousness; it is in the field of our awareness. It is not that our awareness is aware of something other than itself. Whatever we experience is always part of the field of our awareness manifesting as a particular form. Our awareness simply recognizes this change or this arising within it.

If we consider our inner experience as it manifests in the forms of feelings, emotions, thoughts, images, impulses, desires, and so on, we see that these always arise within us as part of us. You could describe them as waves in a field of the same substance or as wave modulations in the same kind of medium. Each wave arises with a certain flavor, texture, color, and quality that makes us experience it as one thing or another. But it is not as though our consciousness were a vacuity, and some object pops out from it. It is not that we are separate, looking at that object as if it were something different from us. Whatever arises is always inseparable from us.

We might not be aware of this if we don't yet know our True Nature. But the moment we know our True Nature, we recognize that everything arises within this True Nature. Everything arises within this field, within this presence, and is no separate from it. So we realize that if we fight anything off that is in our experience, we are dividing ourselves.

INTERFERENCE AS DIVISION

This brings us back to interference and the difficulty we have in keeping our hands off our experience. Interference in our experience always implies a division: We separate ourselves into parts through meddling. So, maybe there is me interfering with my fear. Or me interfering with my love.

Now, this division is recognized, or reveals itself, most clearly when we meddle with an experience, or some aspect of an experience, that we would rather not have or don't feel good about experiencing. Maybe it's something that's scary or painful, or it's something we think is shameful. Perhaps it is something that we feel is too much—too delicate, too sweet, too strong, too powerful—anything that threatens or contradicts what we take ourselves to be. When we are not informed by our True Nature, then whatever it is that we find threatening or objectionable, we tend to oppose or reject. We want to fight it off, to push it away or push against it. We don't want to feel it or we don't want to feel it fully. This tendency to fight with ourselves and the elements of our experience is what we usually call resistance.

Sometimes we don't even want to be aware of what's bothering us, we don't want to know it is there. In these situations, it doesn't matter whether it's something positive, negative, painful, pleasurable, expanded, or contracted emerging in our consciousness. If we are not familiar with it or are scared of it or feel bad about it, we don't want to be aware of it. So we end up opposing something that hasn't even manifested yet. We resist it.

We dull our awareness and thicken it in a manner that opposes and pushes away whatever element is arising in our experience that we prefer not to have. And when we do that, it becomes very difficult just to be present. How are we going to be there, how are we going to be ourselves, if we are fighting something in our experience?

We are trying to divide ourselves; yet, as we have seen, we are indivisible. We are trying to partition ourselves, but our consciousness doesn't have parts. So, all that happens is that we get thick and dull, and our awareness loses its lightness and lucidity and clarity. In fact, our normal awareness has already lost its clarity and lucidity because we are dividing ourselves in so many ways automatically, consciously or unconsciously.

THE NATURE OF RESISTANCE

The stance of the ego-self that doesn't know its nature is to fight some experiences and hold on to others. The ego-self has preferences for what should happen and shouldn't happen, according to its ideal of what we believe is enlightened or not, and what we think is pleasurable or painful. We have all kinds of value and judgment standards about what's good and what's bad, what is scary and what is not. Some of this is conscious, some of it is unconscious, and much of it divides us within. This division creates a kind of war, like a resistance movement within us, whereas our True Nature is inherently undivided and indivisible.

When you are resisting, you are basically resisting yourself. It is a kind of self-resistance. Instead of being with yourself, you are resisting being with yourself. Instead of being yourself, you are resisting being yourself. That is what it means to resist our True Nature. The ego experience, which is by its nature not an experience of simply being ourselves, implies resistance to being.

The moment we take the posture of ego, of identification with our history, it implies resistance. There is no such thing as ego with no resistance, and the ultimate resistance is the resistance to simply being, the resistance to our True Nature. And that's because ego is always trying to do one thing or another, and True Nature isn't doing anything. It just is. It is nature. It is luminous presence.

The nature of ego itself is an ongoing resistance to what is. Even just manifesting as ego implies that we are resisting our nature, because if we didn't resist our nature we would instantly *be* our nature. So, the fact that we are not experiencing ourselves as our True Nature, the fact that we are not this spacious presence, implies resistance.

The resistance can be quite subtle, and of course, there are many reasons for it. It might be that we don't believe that we are our True Nature. We believe instead that who we are is the one who is resisting, and we are attempting to preserve our identity. It might be that allowing ourselves to feel our True Nature would threaten us too much by bringing all kinds of vulnerabilities, fears, or insecurities into the open. In fact, truly being is a kind of death. I talk about things such as resistance and how to be allowing, but to really be without resistance means ego death, ultimately.

Resistance happens in many ways and can be explicit or implicit. Explicit resistance occurs when some experience we don't want arises or is about to arise, and we defend against it by thickening, contracting, dulling ourselves, or pushing against what is there. For example, a hurt is arising, and you say, "No, it's too much; I don't want to feel that." Our consciousness then thickens to push it away, to close it down. There is a direct rejection, denial, or pushing against our experience or some element of it.

On the other hand, sometimes it happens that resistance is implicit or indirect. In that case, we don't try to avoid or stop feeling the objectionable part of our experience—we attempt to manipulate it. For instance, we may try to control our experience or direct it or want it to be something different. We may believe that we are accepting our experience and trying to work with it, but we can't do that without resisting what it is, without fighting off what we are experiencing. We know this must be the case, because if we are not fighting, or resisting, we are spacious—we are allowing whatever is happening to just be as it is.

WORKING WITH RESISTANCE IN PRACTICE

Since most of the time you cannot just be yourself—you cannot be real—you will find yourself resisting and interfering a lot. However, if it should happen that you *can* be real, let that happen. Otherwise it would be resistance again. Whatever is happening is happening. If you happen to be open and present, and things are arising and naturally transforming and freeing themselves from a contracted condition and revealing their underlying lightness and luminosity, that is wonderful. If not, continue to do your best not to judge the things that are arising or do anything with them, because True Nature itself will transform them. True Nature might transform them by revealing their story or meaning. We call the revelation of this story the process of inquiry. We will have much more to say about this process throughout this book.

When I say that resistance is contraindicated in inner practice, I remind you that I am not saying that you should never engage in a resistance movement in the sense of taking appropriate action regarding external circumstances. Remember the rotten peach. What I am referring to is nonresistance within ourselves, within our own field of awareness of experience.

It takes a subtle and full understanding of our own field of experience and of how to live harmoniously within it to understand what to do with an external force. In the meantime, we can only do our best until we get to that point. The more we understand how we respond to what is arising within us, the easier it becomes to learn how to deal with what is arising outside of us, so to speak. (At some point, we recognize that whatever happens is not really outside of us.)

When we are pushing against our experience, fighting it off, it doesn't have the opportunity or the space to be itself. And if it doesn't have the chance to be itself, it doesn't have the chance to unfold. And if it doesn't have the chance to unfold, it doesn't have the opportunity to reveal its nature. So it continues to be whatever manifestation initially arose. In other words, resisting something is one good way to preserve it in the form that we experienced it to begin with. We resist, hoping to get rid of it, but what we are actually doing is encapsulating it and keeping it in its original form or expression.

So, as you see, resistance is futile! Everything that initially appears to have its own identity, its own reality, at some point will be absorbed again into the indivisible unity of True Nature.

Resistance implies a division inside of us. It signals that we are not recognizing that what is arising is a manifestation of our own consciousness, of our own awareness. When hatred arises in us, for example, or fear, it is our soul, our consciousness, taking that form at that time for a reason we perhaps don't understand yet. If we are able to allow the fear or hate, embrace it, hold it, and feel it fully in its totality—in all its texture, color, and vividness—we will give it the space to be itself. And that will happen naturally because it is the nature of our True Nature to move, to unfold, to illuminate itself, and to reveal what it is about. And as our experience reveals what it is about, it will at some point reveal its True Nature because each experience we have is somehow related to our True Nature. And by understanding it, seeing the truth, and following the thread of truth, we are following that connection to True Nature.

TRUE NATURE IS UNDIVIDED
BUT ALLOWS DIVISION

As we have seen, resistance implies an inner division. It is possible to confront the division itself, to see through the duality, but for most of us, that is not a small step. In fact, it is a huge step—or maybe about the ten thousandth average-sized step—on the path. Most of us still need to take the first step, which is just to allow what is happening, just to let that be. Even though we feel the division and duality, we need to allow that duality. Saying, "No, this isn't right; it's dual, it's divided" is a form of resistance; it is taking a position of pushing away what is.

Do you think True Nature is going to do that to duality, to divisiveness? No. True Nature says, "Oh, division . . . interesting, let's find out about that" and just stays with it, allowing the divisiveness to be and inviting it to reveal itself. "Tell me more about yourself. This duality is an interesting phenomenon. I didn't know I could do that. I know myself to be completely indivisible—but look, here is a division. Isn't that amazing! I must be really creative! I can make myself appear as something different from my real nature. This surpasses all special effects. I am not only morphing, I am actually separating out parts of myself."

You might have heard of fictional beings called changelings, or shapeshifters, which are entities that can alter their form at will. You might perceive them as a human being in one moment, as a bird the next, and as a table or a plant or a cloud after that. But in the process, they don't break up into parts and change those; they shift from one complete form into the next. But we as changelings can actually change in such a way that our manifestation appears as two or three things—often in different places in the field of our consciousness. You've probably heard of the psychic capacity called bilocation, right? We do it all the time.

Though True Nature can manifest infinite possibilities, including the experience of inner conflict and division, it is not in its nature to separate something out and fight it off. This is because of True Nature's indivisible oneness. True Nature is not designed for division and conflict; it can't do that. Only its manifestations can appear to separate.

So, instead of a thickening and a bristly fighting attitude toward what is arising in us, our practice shows the importance of the spacious kind of allowing that comes from a place of no division, the openness of our True Nature. We might not be aware of that place of no division, because that is not where we are, that is not what is arising in our experience. But we can remember and learn by recognizing our resistance. Recognizing it, we don't need to go along with it. We can learn to be spacious by being aware of the resistance, being present with it, feeling what it is like and being curious about it.

START BY ALLOWING RESISTANCE

When I say, "Be spacious, allow what is happening out of a spacious attitude," I don't mean that you should deliberately try to create for yourself the sensation or the experience of spaciousness. That might or might not happen by itself, depending on what is there. What I mean is that you include whatever is happening in your awareness; you don't resist it. If what is happening is resistance and thickness, then that is where you are. You can be at peace with thickness, allowing it to happen, letting it be as thick as it wants to be, feeling that thickness as much as possible. So inquiring into it means delving into it and experiencing it fully. The attitude with which you approach your experience is a lot more important than getting to any particular state of consciousness.

Of course, the thickness is a kind of resistance, an attitude that is not allowing, not spacious. So just be aware of that. The idea is to notice it first, and as you notice it, to allow it and let it emerge even more. If it gets thicker, it might be that more thickness is what needs to arise. It needs to become itself as fully as possible until you become a completely thick kind of presence. When you get that thick, many of your capacities are not available because they get clogged. That is fine. Then the only thing left is the awareness itself. So be it.

And so you continue to inquire into your experience. And inquiry does not necessarily mean you have to do something or ask a specific question. It is more like observing with curiosity, "I am feeling thick. I am so thick that I don't even know what is going on. Who knows what this is? I really don't like it. I wish I weren't thick." All of this is included in the inquiry. So if you recognize that you really don't like it, that you'd rather feel delicate and fine, you are recognizing some kind of resistance that might be part of the thickness. That is okay, too. Everything needs to be included.

Whatever it is, welcome it, embrace it. And that doesn't mean that you need to love it. It is understandable that you don't like feeling thick. But not liking it is not the same thing as pushing against it, trying to get rid of it, or judging it.

From the perspective of True Nature, it is natural to be spacious, to be light, to be playful instead of glum when engaging our experience. It is important to recognize that we can have the attitude of being interested in any kind of experience. That means not just allowing it but actually inviting it. If we recognize ourselves as being resistant, glum, and thick, we start with that. It's where we are, so we let ourselves be there and invite it to reveal itself.

So now we come back full circle to remember once again that our practice is to be real. It's always about being ourselves, no matter where we are. Most of us don't know how to be real, how to be ourselves, and we can't just turn some switch on to make that happen. So, what do we do? If we remember the way True Nature works, we have a way to do our practice. Let's review what we've discovered thus far.

- The best approach to being real is to learn to be where we are, because where we are is what is already happening.
- Whatever we are experiencing at any time is part of True Nature, part of our presence, part of our consciousness, part of our awareness.
- True Nature is unable to resist anything. It is not in our True Nature to separate something out and fight it off. It is not designed to do that.
- True Nature manifests its freedom by being inherently spacious and light. It is a spaciousness that feels weightless and functions as an invitation for things to arise and to be themselves and in that way to reveal themselves fully and completely.
- We don't need to go along with the tendency to resist our experience. We can learn to be spacious by being aware of the resist-

ance, being present with the resistance, feeling what it is like, and being curious about it.

- If we are able to allow our experience—to embrace it, hold it, and feel it fully, rather than rejecting it or trying to change it—we give it the space to be itself. Then it will naturally unfold because that is the nature of our True Nature.

- As our experience illuminates itself and reveals what it is about, it will at some point reveal our True Nature, because each experience we have is somehow related to our True Nature.

- By understanding and seeing the truth in our experience and following the thread of that truth, we are following the path to our True Nature.

EXPLORATION SESSION

Inviting Allowing into the Moment

True Nature is interested in its own revelations because it loves to reveal itself; it is its nature to manifest. This is happening all the time, but we can engage it as a particular practice. We call it inquiry when we attend to and explore any process that is naturally occurring. When we are aware of our experience, consciously engaging it, and inviting its unfoldment through our immediate presence, that is inquiry.

Spend fifteen minutes exploring your experience as it arises moment to moment. The practice is to allow yourself to be where you are. Recognize whatever your experience is and let it be. If you are simply aware of it, with curiosity and interest, it will begin to reveal itself, and it will flow and move to the next moment. If you continue to let it be as it is, all the while remaining interested in what it is, the changes in experience become a process, an unfoldment, an inner inquiry, and discovery.

When you have finished, take ten minutes to reflect on the presence of both resistance and allowing in your inquiry. When was there resistance and when was there more allowing? In this way, you can recognize for yourself what kinds of feelings tend to arise that draw you into rejection, avoidance, manipulation, control, or any other kind of active meddling. Becoming more aware of when you allow and when you resist will help you learn to appreciate the difference.

CHAPTER 5

Opening to Ourselves

WE CANNOT GIVE ANY REASON for the fact that we love being ourselves. We can come up with reasons, but none of them will be true because there really aren't any; we just inherently love ourselves and our nature. And in our True Nature, we love everything and everybody. That love is simply part of reality. When we feel that we are being ourselves, we feel real. We feel intimate with ourselves, close to ourselves, but not close in the sense of there being two who are close to each other. It is more a sense of nearness of our own beingness, without any distance. That absence of distance, or of dissociation, has in it a sense of intimacy and of relaxation, of being settled in one's being.

And we are not necessarily trying to describe that sense of being that we are experiencing; it doesn't matter what quality or dimension of Being is manifesting. We are simply settled in our real self, instead of fabricating ourselves or *trying* to be ourselves or being in reaction to one thing or another.

THE INTIMACY OF
BEING OURSELVES

Being ourselves is a delight. It is an intimacy; it is a genuineness, a preciousness. It is indescribable how satisfying it feels to us. But what I want to point to here is the fact that being ourselves implies an openness, a kind of gentleness. When we are being ourselves, we feel intimate, we feel close to ourselves. Our heart is open, our mind is clear, our soul is settled; there is no sense of thickness or inner agitation or fighting within ourselves. We experience an inner unity that feels peaceful, relaxed, contented. And whether we are feeling one specific quality or aspect of our being or we are feeling True Nature in its transcendence or boundlessness, we enjoy a delightful freedom and satisfaction.

As we progress through these teachings together, we are learning to approach that delight, to practice in such a way that we find ourselves in that condition. Thus far, we have seen that, in simplest terms, the key is to find out where we are and just let ourselves be there, with awareness and with understanding. We have seen that where we are in any moment is the closest thing to our True Nature because our current condition—regardless of what it is—is our present link to that True Nature.

Now when I say "approach," it is just a manner of speaking; we are not trying to approach anything. I may describe a way to approach the condition of being ourselves, but it is an approach that is not taking us anywhere. We are just accepting what is. We are recognizing what is happening and how we are experiencing ourselves, and we are at peace with that. We are so much at peace that nothing gets in the way of us being aware of our experience, being comfortable as we are fully aware of it and recognizing what it is about totally.

In previous chapters, we have been looking at various obstacles and impediments to just finding where we are and being where we are. We have become more aware of the attempts we make to manipulate and direct our experience in one way or another. We see that this is because we think that our experience is not okay as it is. We have discussed the specific meddling we engage in that resists our experience by actually opposing it, pushing against it, or trying to fight it off. We have recognized this resistance as a thickening of our consciousness or our awareness that makes it impossible to feel the intimacy, the genuineness, and the warmth of authenticity in being ourselves. Now we want to add to our understanding by looking at another form of meddling with our experience that also happens by thickening our consciousness: inner defensiveness.

THE DEFENSE OF
INNER HARDENING

Resistance is an active mode of inner coercion that reflects or overlaps with a more passive form of inner manipulation—our defensiveness. As with defense, resistance frequently implies a need to protect ourselves. Sometimes we resist because we don't like what we are experiencing; we'd prefer something else, so we judge what actually is. Perhaps we are angry at what is happening in us. Or we are tired of it. But much of the time, we resist because we feel we need to protect ourselves. And protection is the basic motivation for putting up inner defenses.

When we perceive a real danger or threat, or when we imagine one, we tend to harden ourselves for self-protection. But by hardening ourselves, we are not only thickening our consciousness, we are also making it stiff and solid, and it becomes impossible to experience that delicacy, that gentleness and intimacy, of being ourselves. That hardening reaction—building a wall of protection and separation—which becomes an impediment against finding where we are, is the ego's basic mode of defense. Ego is based mainly on defenses—defending itself against dangers—inner and outer, imaginary and real. Ego does not really exist without its defenses.

But when we are trying to defend ourselves internally, we are in some sense trying to run away. We are trying to hide. We are trying to isolate, to separate ourselves, to put a distance between us and the danger. And that happens in many ways. One strategy is to create a passive structure of defense. We can do this by erecting inner walls against our experience of fear, against our perception of danger, against feeling the possibility of threat or attack or pain. Those walls can be inside of us separating different parts of us—such as our heart and our genitals, our consciousness and our unconscious—or they can be between us and what we perceive as the outside.

But the walls are just one manifestation of the ego's defensive tendency. Ego-defensiveness also manifests in other ways, such as hiding, running away, isolating oneself, contracting, or restraining oneself from showing up fully. These are all ways of resisting what is present in our experience. The intent is to avoid being open because being open means leaving oneself undefended and unprotected. Being open means being ourselves, and we believe that being ourselves is dangerous because then we are vulnerable to all kinds of threats.

HUMAN NEED FOR
SELF-PROTECTION

So, to be ourselves, which means to be our True Nature, is to be in simplicity, without defenses. Even just being where we are without fighting it means that we are not trying to protect ourselves against one kind of danger or another. And that is a difficult thing for human beings. This difficulty is related not only to how we were raised in childhood, but also to our genetic history. To a great extent, human beings as a race have evolved in very harsh environments where danger was a clear and present reality. In time, we learned that to have any possibility at all of being ourselves, we have to survive, and that to survive requires protecting ourselves. The fact that self-protection is necessary for survival has been conditioned in us, not only as external forms of defense such as armies and police, but also as internal forms of defense such as building inner walls.

Suppose you are actually being faced with an external danger, that somebody is out to get you. How does building an inner wall help? How does not feeling our fear help? Feeling our fear or weakness or sadness might be difficult when confronted from the outside, but being in touch with those feelings grounds our experience in reality. To wall off our feelings will only cause our external defense to be more hard and rigid and thus less responsive to the danger.

And what happens when we put up walls against what we perceive as inner danger, the real cause of the ego's defensiveness? What else could our inner dangers be but our own feelings, our own thoughts, our own memories, our own states? We are afraid of ourselves, really, of the manifestations of our being, of our consciousness.

As we know from modern psychology, the ego has a huge amount of past experience that it keeps unconscious through active mental defenses that are themselves mostly beyond our awareness. All kinds of mental operations are constantly going on to protect us from experiencing one thing or another. Our unconscious is teeming with memories and feelings, but most people think of it as teeming with lurking dangers and demons. People talk about their inner demons, their dark side. What is the dark side? It is a scary, dark place inside of you from which you think your personal demons are going to come and gobble you up. What are you going to do to stop them? Many people harden themselves so much that they don't feel anything. Then no inner demons can get them!

We can be humorous about it, but it is actually a serious situation. And it is a real one, because when we were little, we were delicate and many things were truly dangerous for us. We couldn't tolerate much of what we were experiencing; we could not comprehend it, and our nervous system was not equipped to deal with it at that age. So we had no way to take care of ourselves mentally or emotionally. We were naturally vulnerable in our openness. The reality in our early years was that we did need to protect and defend ourselves because we couldn't handle the situation. It was as simple as that. If we had a loving, caring, supportive environment, that helped a lot, but even that couldn't do the whole job.

The human soul, when it is in touch with its nature, is open. In that openness, it is vulnerable. But being vulnerable only means being open in relation to danger. If there is no danger, open doesn't feel vulnerable. It just feels carefree and easy. But if danger is present when you are open, you feel scared, a little shaky, and vulnerable.

As children, we were open and delicate and gentle, which meant that we lacked hardness, we lacked defenses, and we lacked a shield around us. But when we felt exposed and afraid, we learned to build those shields to protect ourselves, to defend ourselves from the environment around us. So now, as adults, we continue to put up walls and shields to stop the environment from affecting us. In order to protect ourselves from outside dangers, we stop ourselves from feeling vulnerable by closing down our own feelings, our own sensations, our own imagination.

I am not saying that physical self-protection is unimportant or unnecessary. But hardening ourselves internally is not truly helpful in accomplishing this. It is an illusory protection because it does not affect the outside danger at all; it only diminishes our internal awareness and aliveness. It was only helpful when we had no way as children to protect ourselves externally, and we used our internal defenses to diminish the impact of overwhelming feelings when the external cause could not be stopped.

That is why it is not easy to learn to really be ourselves. It is simple, but it is complicated by the fact that to be ourselves means being open. To be where we are without doing anything about it means that we don't do anything to protect ourselves, we don't put up walls, we don't hide ourselves. It means that we are really out there. When I say "out there," I don't mean out there in the middle of the highway. "Out there" might be in your own bedroom, by yourself, without any defenses. Maybe you think somebody is going to jump out at you from the TV! So being out there by yourself might make you feel naked and you get scared.

We end up being paranoid in some sense and afraid of our own experience. So, if we are scared of our experience and even of the possibilities that might arise in our experience, how are we going to learn to be real, to be ourselves? How are we going to learn to see exactly where we are and be there—abide where we are—when that might include experiencing danger or perhaps a condition that we think will invite danger? "If I let myself be where I am, what will happen to me? I will be jumped on." That's why we automatically defend ourselves. You don't have to be walking around in an unsafe neighborhood to be afraid for your own safety. You could be in your own room and still not feel safe. What I am saying is that you are defending yourself there, too.

Defenses have become so institutionalized, so much a part of our character and personality, that at some point we don't recognize that they are there. They have become part of our internal structure. But in our attempts to protect ourselves from real or imagined danger, our awareness becomes diminished. That is because being completely aware would mean being aware of all the things that scare us or might hurt us or that we are ashamed of. So we defend against them and stop being aware. Much of the time, we are defending ourselves against reality; and it is not against reality as much as it is against our own experience. The implication for our practice is that we can recognize and understand this and be aware that we will encounter these things as we continue to practice being where we are.

DEFENSIVENESS
AND VULNERABILITY

Let's review a few key points about defensiveness and then see what we can understand about the process of its transformation. This process includes encountering the vulnerability that inevitably comes up as we become aware of how we defend ourselves:

- As we practice—which entails inquiring into what is going on, recognizing our experience, being where we are, abiding in it, and learning to be ourselves—we encounter a stance of defensiveness that we become more and more conscious of.

- That defensiveness is a barrier against our unconscious, but also against much of our potential, because it is a defense against experience, a defense against the expansion of awareness, a defense against being present, a defense against being real.
- When a defense is pushed against or challenged, it changes from a passive wall to an active resistance against what is arising, a resistance against recognizing what we think is—or could become—dangerous or threatening.
- The defensiveness is a hardening and a thickening of our consciousness, creating walls within us.
- If we recognize those walls and are able to understand them, they begin to transform and start to come down.
- As those defenses gradually dissolve, as those walls come down, we will have the feeling of no protection for a while. Without the walls, when we still do not feel the security of being ourselves, we will experience that as defenselessness. And that defenselessness will feel like a kind of vulnerability, a trembling emotional condition of the heart that makes us feel quite delicate.
- That delicacy, that trembling, means that we are open but we still believe that there is danger. So we are still tentative, a little cautious, a little reactive. That is because as we are approaching the delicacy of being ourselves, the delicacy of intimacy; we are approaching it by letting go of the walls, and we are still not used to being in that openness.
- Our defensiveness at some point becomes a wall against vulnerability. So to learn to be real, to learn to be ourselves, we need to come to terms with our vulnerability.

VULNERABILITY:
THE DOOR TO TRUE NATURE

What does it mean to come to terms with our vulnerability? It means recognizing it and seeing it for what it is. It means identifying all the beliefs we have in our unconscious about real and imagined dangers and the way we have been trying to deal with them. It means seeing how our defensiveness doesn't work, how it only cuts us off from ourselves and from our resources.

It also means being able, at some point, to appreciate the vulnerability we feel, because vulnerability means openness. If my consciousness is vulnerable, that means I am also vulnerable to the manifestations of my True Nature. If I defend myself, I am not open to my True Nature and its manifestation. I am not only protecting myself from other people, I begin to protect myself from True Nature itself, with all its qualities.

The wonderful thing is that vulnerability becomes the door to intimacy, to being ourselves, to being real, to being where we are. But for that to happen, we have to be willing to be vulnerable to what is. Being vulnerable means that our soul is open for things to arise in it. It is not defended.

If it has walls, it is preventing things from arising; it is not allowing the dynamism of our Being to transform our condition. This means that it will only transform in ways that don't feel threatening—in other words, ways that are familiar to us. But being vulnerable allows our soul to transform into something new and unfamiliar, and that at first is scary—which means we will feel undefended.

As human beings, we have always been vulnerable. Our natural state is to be undefended. In fact, the defensiveness of human beings, the sense of security that ego constructs by building defensive walls to hide or camouflage itself, is arrogant and even delusional. Because when it comes to real danger, we are vulnerable all the time; we can be damaged easily. For example, we are quite vulnerable physically. A little virus that you can't even see can get you, and the next day you are on your back and you can't even move.

But our vulnerability is also the quality of our humanness. It is a heart quality of openness, of gentleness, that is needed for us to recognize where we are and to abide there. We cannot truly recognize where we are without that gentleness, that humanness, that humility. But that means we will find ourselves in a vulnerable condition.

Vulnerability in the face of danger feels frightening, but in the absence of danger, vulnerability can simply mean feeling naturally, undefendedly yourself.

So we have a dilemma. We are scared, we want to protect ourselves, but at the same time we want to be real. How are we going to solve this paradox? How do we protect ourselves against danger and still be real? We come back to the peach . . . You do things to take care of yourself. You get professional health care as you need it, you brush your teeth, you take reasonable precautions if you are walking through an unsafe neighborhood, you don't hang out with gangs, and so on. You use your intelligence to do what is necessary—you defend yourself physically if that is called for—but inside you remain vulnerable, open, supple, gentle. And you begin to appreciate vulnerability as a human quality that gives us the openness to reality, to perception, to our True Nature in all of its manifestations.

We cannot be ourselves if we don't experience that vulnerability, because vulnerability is just the beginning of experiencing the gentleness and the exquisiteness of being genuine. In time, we learn that we can feel completely undefended without it feeling scary, without feeling that we need to defend ourselves, without the need for those inner walls.

DEFENSIVENESS AS
EGO BOUNDARY

The issue of defenses is a deep one because putting up walls implies that there is somebody who is putting up those walls around himself or herself. The walls we construct ultimately become our defining boundaries. They define who we are inside, and then we put walls around that self to protect it from danger. So we cannot be completely free of defensiveness as long as we are holding on to the definition of our boundaries—what we believe defines us as a human being. At some point, we recognize that our defended condition is tied in with our boundedness, and that this sense of boundedness doesn't respect our True Nature—because True Nature has no size and no shape; it is without boundaries.

Looking at the relationship between ego boundaries and our definition of self as we have just done is a way to recognize how deep our defenses go. Resistance operates in a similar way to putting up defenses. Thus, having no resistance and having no defenses both mean ego death at some point—the dissolution of the boundaries that define us as individuals. And we create many other kinds of defenses and walls and hard places to protect ourselves from experiencing certain parts of ourselves and our history. We defend against certain situations, against feeling the implications of those situations and what we perceive about them. So when we perceive something but we don't want to let ourselves experience what it makes us feel, where does that put us? Immediately we feel we need to defend, to create an inner boundary that allows us to see things without having to feel how they affect us.

Psychologists have made long lists of the kinds of defenses people engage in. Projection, identification, and repression, for example, are different ways to defend ourselves against perceiving reality and being totally in the moment, against feeling ourselves completely. They are ways to distance ourselves from the intimacy and the immediacy of just being ourselves. The purpose might be to protect our vulnerability, our genuineness, our reality, our sense of self; but in each case, we dissociate ourselves from the preciousness we want to protect. We might have felt it necessary as children, but it usually no longer is. However, self-protection has become habitual, institutionalized in our character.

Only by opening ourselves to what is present in our experience—especially our tendency to defend ourselves—can we challenge our fear of being real. The more we see our defensiveness and understand it, the more we invite in the tender, intimate vulnerability of our souls that is hidden behind the walls. It is this vulnerability that allows our true humanness to reveal itself in the simplicity of being ourselves.

EXPLORATION SESSION

Exploring Vulnerability in the Present

This exercise will help clarify the relationship between vulnerability and being open to your experience in the moment. Vulnerability is a state of consciousness in which we feel open, delicate, sensitive, alive, undefended, and intimate with ourselves. But it also tends to be associated with fear and danger. Vulnerability is not a state we generally live our life from.

As you pay attention to yourself in the moment, notice whether you experience yourself as being open or not. If not, what is stopping you from feeling open—to your thoughts, to your feelings, to your sensations, to how you are impacted by your experience? If you are more open to the specifics of your inner experience, does that bring a sense of vulnerability? If so, what is feeling vulnerable like for you? Is it okay? Is it tolerable?

If you find vulnerability arising as you explore, notice how the sense of vulnerability manifests in your body, your thoughts, your emotions, your voice, as you explore each aspect of your experience. This may include qualities such as gentleness, delicacy, fragility, fear, trembling, receptivity, sensitivity.

You can develop this contemplation further by exploring any situations that make you feel vulnerable. As you do this, consider how vulnerability and fear are related in your experience. Do they always go together? Remember that vulnerability can mean freedom and openness as well.

CHAPTER 6

Cultivating a Bold Vulnerability

B Y NOW, YOU PROBABLY HAVE experienced various types of obstacles and impediments arising as you continue your inner practice of finding where you are and abiding there. You may be coming to the understanding that the obstacles to being where you are turn out to be the same as the obstacles to being yourself and that those are the same as the obstacles to reality and to realization.

Understanding how these obstacles arise within your experience is a major factor in our practice. But there are additional factors that, once understood, can also make our practice simpler and easier.

As we have seen, most of the time we don't know exactly what's happening with us. We know scattered bits and pieces, but it is difficult to see how they fit into one coherent manifestation. And we notice that even when we pay attention and are aware of our experience, we don't automatically know where we are.

Knowing where we are requires some clarity. It takes some inquiry. To further our understanding, a specific discrimination can be made to support our practice of finding where we are and letting ourselves be. That is, we can learn how to differentiate our experience into two parts: the primary component and the secondary components.

The primary component is the central event—the main thing that is actually arising in our personal experience at any given moment. And that can be anything. It can be a feeling or emotion, such as a state of joy or love or dread. It can be a sense of deficiency or feeling like an empty shell. It can be some kind of activity or perhaps an imagining. So the primary component is what is actually emerging in the field of our consciousness, in the field of our soul.

The secondary components are the reactions and responses to the primary component, to the central event. There is generally one primary component, but there may be many secondary ones. We experience the main event as it arises, and we also experience commentaries, reactions, and attitudes to that primary event.

Those responses can be all kinds of things—for example, self-congratulation or pride about what we are feeling or embarrassment and guilt about feeling this way instead of some other way. It could be excitement about our condition or avoidance of it, or a thought process that interferes with or shuts down what's happening. So we have what is arising as the central event plus our reaction or attitude toward it. Maybe we don't like it, or we want more, or we judge it or want to change it, or it makes us feel sad, or perhaps we feel that our experience makes us better than someone else.

The fact that many thoughts, feelings, activities, and impulses arise in us in response to the central event makes it difficult to see where we are. To know where we are, we need to find out what is centrally arising. What's the primary component? Much of the time we are trapped in the secondary components, and we cannot separate those from the primary event. Is what I'm experiencing the primary event, or am I experiencing my fear or judgment of it or my thought process around it? Can I separate these responses from the event itself?

The relationship of primary and secondary components in our experience can be likened to the phenomenon called a black hole. A black hole is an area in space that appears black or empty because in that location, a nuclear event of such mass and intensity is occurring that nothing can escape the gravitational pull of the event—no matter of any kind, and not even light. Each black hole has what is called an event horizon, which exists at a certain distance from the center of the hole. Anything that reaches the event horizon disappears from view. Scientists are discovering that the event horizon is a very busy place. All kinds of things happen there because of the black hole. As a metaphor for our inner process, the event horizon is where the secondary components are. The actual event that is happening—the primary component of our experience—is beyond, inside the black hole, at the center.

In our human experience, we tend to be afraid to go beyond the event horizon, because we imagine that we're going to be pulled into some sort of inner black hole. Consider your experience and you will see that the focus of your attention is generally on judgments of the primary event—fears about what it means, upset or disturbance over what we think caused it, or efforts to change it. To simply be in touch with the primary component of our experience seems inconceivable. If that central event is an emotion, we may feel it will go on forever or that we will be overwhelmed by it. If it is an energetic experience, we may feel that we will be lost without our story or ideas about it. If it is a difficulty, we may feel that we will be stuck with it forever if we don't focus on resolving it. In our fear of the "black hole" of our experience, we distract ourselves with associations and reactions, rather than just being with the primary experience.

But to be where we are, we need to see what the main event is. Being where we are in the present means not only *seeing* where the event is but *being* where it is. If we remain at the event horizon with only the secondary manifestations, we're not being where we truly are; we are engaged in the secondary processes that are a reaction or response, that are tangential to where we are.

CHANGING COMPONENTS
IN THE SPIRITUAL JOURNEY

The nature of where we are and the nature of the secondary components are determined by where we are in our spiritual journey. Our experience will have different manifestations depending on the stage we are at in the unfolding of our soul.

In the earliest stage of the journey—when we are learning to become more present to where we are—our experience and our inquiry operate within the normal range of sensations, feelings, emotions, thoughts, images, and reactions. These are the usual elements of experience for the ordinary self. Although we keep practicing being present, and we keep practicing inquiry, being present at this stage means that we are in one personality state or another—perhaps experiencing a deficiency or an identification or a particular pattern of behavior or some kind of emotional or mental or physical state. We have not yet reached the discovery of essential presence, so our journey is *toward* presence.

The next stage begins once we have discovered and recognized presence as an expression of our True Nature with its pure sense of here-ness, its authenticity, its is-ness, its immaculateness. Here our journey continues with an awareness of presence. We still exist as we have known ourselves—as an ego-self—but we now have a more or less continuous experience of presence, arising as the various qualities and dimensions of our True Nature.

In the third stage, we are journeying *in* presence, not just *with* presence. Now presence has moved to center stage, and it is the field within which all of our experience arises. This is what we call nonduality, and our practice becomes nondual practice. Presence here is the ground, the nature, of everything in its essence and its manifestation.

Let's take a look at how the nature of the primary and secondary components of our experience differ according to what stage of the journey we are in. In the first stage, the primary component and the secondary component tend to be similar. The primary component might be an emotion, such as fear or terror or happiness, or it could be a sense of deficiency or a particular pattern or self-image. The secondary components might include fear or rejection of the sense of deficiency, judgment or shame about a particular self-image, or commentaries and plans about whatever else might be arising.

We learn through the process of inquiry how to discern the two types of components and distinguish them from one another. First, we need to recognize a reaction as a secondary component and not as the primary event. The recognition of any secondary component makes clear what the primary component is. That's why we always want to include both in our inquiry. Because if we don't see our reactions, we'll never know what the primary component is.

As soon as we identify the primary component and can be fully present with it—recognize it completely, feel it fully, intimately hold it—what is arising begins to unfold and change. We might find out that it has become a secondary component to something more primary. Let's say our primary component is terror. When we feel the terror fully, we might recognize that underneath it is a sense of disintegration. The experience of disintegration then becomes the primary component and the terror becomes a secondary reaction. And the process keeps going, as other, deeper, primary components emerge.

In the second stage of the journey, the primary component is usually essential presence itself. When we inquire into where we are, we are asking, "What is the particular quality of presence arising in this moment? Is it strength? Is it power? Is it compassion? Is it boundless awareness?" The secondary component, then, will be the ego structures and patterns and the self-images and reactions that arise in relation to that particular quality of presence.

In this stage, unfolding is already happening. The center of our experience is presence, and the unfolding is the flow of the presence arising as one quality after another. As that happens, the secondary components arise—the issues, the ego structures, images, or patterns that are in reaction. We need to recognize these so we don't become disconnected from the primary component, which is the presence itself. Often our experience will move farther from or closer to the center of presence as we confront what is arising in us. But the sense of presence always provides the thread for knowing where we are. When we're experiencing the presence, being where we are means not just knowing or experiencing it, but being it. Thus with presence, it becomes very easy to know what it means to be where we are.

When we get to the third stage, the primary component is the presence, and the secondary components are the particular manifestations that arise within that presence. Everything other than pure presence itself is a secondary component. Secondary components can include our feelings, our body, the environment with its shapes and forms, various qualities of light, or inner forms such as ideas, visions, or essential aspects. (These aspects are the various facets of our True Nature—such as clarity, strength, will, or compassion—which arise as discriminated qualities in response to the needs of our situation.) All the shapes and forms—the manifestations—become the secondary components, and they're always changing. The presence is always the ground. Being ourselves means being the presence, but the presence here is inseparable from all that is arising within it. That is because everything that arises in our experience is a form or expression that this presence takes.

So let's summarize and review the main distinctions we have identified thus far in this chapter.

The two components of experience are:

1. The primary component: the central event that is arising in our personal experience
2. The secondary component: our reactions and responses to the central event

The three stages of the journey that determine the nature and unfolding of the primary and secondary components are:

1. The practice of awareness and inquiry deepening toward the discovery of presence

2. The practice of awareness and inquiry constantly revealing presence at the heart of experience
3. Being with inquiry, awareness, and experience as the spontaneous unfolding of presence

As you can surmise from all that has been said, the practice of being where we are is a practice that encompasses all three stages of our journey—the entire inner path we are traveling. It combines the practices of presence, awareness, and inquiry. Thus it encompasses our regular activities in daily life as well as our sitting meditations, and it includes how we practice being ourselves in every situation. All our life experiences are variations of the practice of being where we are with awareness, with presence, and with understanding.

THE OBSTACLE OF AGGRESSION

All obstacles to being ourselves can be divided into three categories: ignorance, desire, and aggression. These major categories are known in many spiritual traditions. They are called the three primary poisons or the three primary roots. Many obstacles can be placed in more than one category. Most obstacles, including those we have explored so far—meddling, resistance, and defense—are a combination of all three. In reality, all three categories are facets of the same thing: they are the three supports of the ego-self, which you can also call the ego life or ego experience.

We have recognized the need for many essential aspects, many capacities, that enable us to see and recognize where we are. In earlier chapters, we have discussed awareness, allowing, vulnerability, steadfastness, the capacity to cease interfering, and others. Whenever we are faced with an obstacle, one or more of these qualities of presence can be of help to us. I want to introduce now two other necessary qualities that complement each other: the aspects of strength and compassion. These two can help us when we are faced with obstacles in the category that the majority of people find the most painful to deal with: aggression.

As we have seen, the main reason we engage in meddling, resistance, and defense is that we're afraid that if we're vulnerable, if we're open, if we allow ourselves to just simply be where we are, we will not be safe. Many people these days blame their insecurity on terrorism in the world. But the actual lack of safety is more a result of the terrorism that is inside our minds—the internal saboteurs. Our primary fear is that if we are open and let ourselves be where we are, we're going to be belittled. We're going to be rejected. We're going to be humiliated. We're going to be attacked. We're going to be judged. We're going to be criticized. We're going to be shamed. We're going to be made to feel guilty.

We're afraid that other people will do these things to us and sometimes that actually happens. But more often, we do these things to ourselves. Have you ever said to yourself, "If I really let myself be vulnerable, I feel so delicate, sweet, and innocent. If people notice that, they will judge me as good for nothing"? Or maybe you've thought, "If I feel that sweet innocence, I'm going to get embarrassed. I'm going to be humiliated. It means I'm not strong. Somebody is going to reject me or shame me." These worries are usually a projection onto other people of our own inner terrorist that's scaring us.

All of these projections are examples of the obstacle of aggression. We normally think that aggression is about people killing or hurting other people. But for people who are on the inner journey, that's only a very small part of it. The primary form of aggression for those on the path is their aggression toward themselves. We don't allow ourselves to be open and vulnerable, to be where we are, because whatever we find as primary in that experience of vulnerability is often connected to a feeling of deficiency, and we might attack the hell out of ourselves for it: "You're no good. You're not enough. You'll never amount to anything."

Right away, we become afraid that somebody is going to think those things about us. But why do you always believe that no matter what, somebody's going to think you're not good enough? Why can't you imagine that they might think something else? Is it likely that everyone on Earth is thinking the same thought—that you're not good enough? Why doesn't it occur to you that some of them will just think you're weird? And that others will think you're naive? No, you believe they will all think you're not good enough.

Obviously, the common factor among all these people is that you are projecting onto them. This is one way that we avoid facing the primary component that is arising in our own experience. We rationalize, defend ourselves, justify ourselves. But to whom are we justifying ourselves? Why do we need to blame anybody? We simply are not comfortable about where we are, but we don't want to feel that, so we make others responsible for our discomfort by projecting onto them our own reaction. Our focus is outward on them instead of inward on what's true about ourselves.

What we're seeing here is the activity of what we call the superego. The superego is a specialized part of our ego structure that has the job of making sure we live up to the standards we learned as children to survive in our families and communities. It does this by various means, including judging, criticizing, advising, warning, encouraging, threatening, and punishing ourselves in reaction to our thoughts, feelings, and actions. The superego is one way that aggression toward ourselves manifests, and it becomes a big obstacle to finding where we are and just being there. It is a major barrier to being ourselves, to being real.

Being real might mean experiencing yourself as immense and powerful, but your superego might think that's unacceptable. It warns you, "You're going to be too much for people. They won't want to be with you. They will abandon you or judge you as too loud or too aggressive."

So we have all these judgments, and we feel humiliated, ashamed, embarrassed, guilty, worthless, deficient. But all of these feelings stem from our own aggression toward ourselves. So when you hear someone say, "Let yourself be where you are," you probably think, "Why would I want to be where I am? I don't want to be anywhere in particular. If I'm somewhere specific, it's usually trouble. Somebody's going to get me." But the who that's going to get you is usually part of your own mind.

So when it comes to finding and being where we are, we need to recognize the secondary reactions that come from the superego— reactions of attack, rejection, humiliation, shame, guilt, belittling, devaluing, comparing, and so on. The superego has many ways to keep us in place, to keep us from where we really are, to keep us this side of the event horizon where we cannot see what is happening in the center of our experience.

WORKING WITH THE SUPEREGO

Because the attacks of the superego are so debilitating, we need to know how to effectively counter them. There are three primary ways to successfully deal with the superego, and they are linked with the three stages of the journey that we discussed earlier.

Stage One: Using the Strength of Aggression

The first way works well during stage one of the journey when our awareness is not strong, our presence is not developed, and our inquiry is not yet skillful. That's when we need to directly defend ourselves, to own up to our aggression and to use its strength and energy to throw the superego out, to create space to be where we are. In this way, we defend ourselves consciously—by using our strength to create space instead of erecting walls, defenses, and resistance to protect us from dangers of the superego.

In the early years of our practice of being where we are, we need to constantly recognize the superego and its ploys and learn how to defend against them. Basically, we need to tell the superego where to go: "Who cares what you think? Go to hell." Okay, so you feel deficient, and the superego keeps insisting that you'll never amount to anything. You can tell it, "Good—if I'm never going to amount to anything, why are you bothering me? Go find somebody else."

This is a way of disengaging, but with strength, with energy, with awareness. The superego wants to fence you in, and you need to expand outward. This kind of defense not only disrupts the superego and silences it, but it also expands our energy. It allows space for us to recognize where we are and to be there without interference.

Stage Two: Using Awareness and Understanding
The second stage of working with the superego begins after we have learned to defend against it with strength, boldness, and aggressiveness. These are energies that we have taken back and owned and therefore can use. Our awareness is now strong and clear, and our inquiry skills are sufficiently developed to prevent a superego attack from confusing us or putting us into a tailspin. At this point, using aggression to defend ourselves is less important; simply recognizing and understanding an attack can counter it. We can often dissolve an attack simply by knowing that the superego is attacking us and understanding why.

During the first stage, understanding alone usually will not work very well, as the long history of psychoanalysis has shown. Psychoanalysts have not found a way to successfully deal with the superegos of many of their patients. After fifteen to twenty years of analysis, people still attack themselves and feel guilty. This is because simply understanding the origins of their superego dynamics—you're feeling this way because of your father . . . it's because your mother did such and such—is rarely sufficient to stop an attack.

At the beginning stages of working with the superego, you don't have enough awareness and presence to be able to explore and understand while under attack. You need to have some space in your experience, which means space from the superego. That's why it's important to learn how to defend yourself with strength. Some people don't want to do that, however, because they're scared of their own aggression, or they are afraid to separate from the attacking inner figures of their parents.

But in the second stage, when we're more established in our presence and our awareness, it is easier to deal with the attacks. By then, they are not as loud or as powerful and are more easily recognized. Recognizing and understanding the superego and its functioning dissolves its attacks. Using awareness and understanding to work with the superego becomes the focus in the second stage.

Stage Three: Using Recognition

Eventually, we come to the third stage of the inner journey, the condition of nondual presence with its manifestations. When the superego arises during this stage, merely recognizing that an attack has been made usually will dissolve it. We don't need to do much beyond that—any work to try to understand why and how the attack occurred is not necessary.

So, to summarize:

- In the first stage of the journey, we need to call on our aggression in the form of strength to separate from and defend against the manipulation of our experience by the superego.
- In the second stage of the journey, recognizing a superego attack and understanding how it works is usually sufficient to dissolve the attack.
- In the third stage of the journey, just recognizing that an attack is in progress is sufficient to stop it.

As we deal with the superego, we learn that the intention of this major coercive agent within us is to try to direct our experience. Basically, the superego is trying to make you feel one thing and not another: "This is acceptable; that is not acceptable. This is okay; that is not okay." But the superego can manifest not only in the form of attacks, but also as positive feedback: a pat on the back, pride in your accomplishments, self-congratulation, or a little bit of ego inflation. What's important to remember is that all inputs by the superego are secondary components—reactions within the event horizon. The main event is what's really happening. If I'm authentically in a condition of realization, why do I need to pat myself on the back? Who's doing that? If I'm feeling proud, who's proud? If I'm getting inflated, what does that mean? What it really means is that I'm going beyond the center and traveling again to the periphery.

So we need to defend ourselves even against so-called positive internal commentary. When the superego tells us that we did a great job, we can say, "Who asked you?" In time, we won't care what it's saying. And eventually, if we are able to deal with the superego in that way, we won't care whether other people approve of us or disapprove of us either. Resistance is futile, but approval and disapproval become irrelevant. They are irrelevant because you are going to be absorbed into the black hole anyway. That's where you can be at peace. This side of the event horizon is where the noise is.

THE NEED FOR COMPASSION

We learn from this brief overview of the superego that the attitude we need to have toward ourselves in our inquiry is not one of harshness. We perceive the harshness of self-directed aggression the more we recognize the superego at work. In time, we come to understand that what's needed is a gentleness and an empathy toward the way we are. If we're feeling weak, we don't tell ourselves things that make us feel bad about that, and we don't judge ourselves. We're understanding, we're kind, we're empathic. If we're feeling deficient, that's not a time to criticize ourselves or compare ourselves with somebody else. It's a time to hold ourselves tenderly.

In time, instead of the superego's harsh criticism, we experience more compassion and warmth, the attunement and empathy of a kind heart. Our inquiry begins to assume more gentleness in the way we perceive and recognize ourselves. We don't just recognize where we are; we recognize where we are with kind, empathic attunement. And our responses become more and more suited to what we need. For example, if we're feeling shame, we don't need to hear from our superego, "Here it comes again . . . you never feel anything else . . . you're always ashamed . . . what's wrong with you?"

What if the inner attitude could shift from "I'm always feeling ashamed; I wish I felt different," to "I'm feeling ashamed and it's really painful"? There's a slight shift, you see? Instead of harshness, there's a gentleness and an implicit compassion that makes us more willing to see exactly where we are and to just be there.

When we are kind to ourselves, there is a warmth in the atmosphere, and we're willing to reveal to ourselves what we truly feel. The compassion is really an empathic recognition of where we are in all its nuances, which brings forth just the right attitude that corresponds to our condition. So, in our example above, there is not only a recognition that it's painful to feel shame, but also a tender warmth in that recognition. We feel much safer to recognize where we are and be there.

THE IMPORTANCE OF COURAGE

Remember that at the beginning of our practice, we need to defend ourselves against the superego, and to do that, we need to bring forth our aggression and our strength. As a matter of fact, in time, simply feeling our strength burns up the superego, without our doing anything to make it happen. However, we recognize that the importance of strength also lies in its function of complementing kindness. We cannot progress on the path with kindness alone, because sometimes what is happening is scary or destabilizing or disorienting. Perhaps where we are is terrifying because what's happening is unknown, totally unfamiliar. Or there's the possibility of pain or of feeling lost or falling apart if we keep going. Then kindness might not be of much help.

That's when we need courage. We need a bold, courageous, adventurous heart to take us where we have never gone. Because that's what the inner journey is—going where we haven't gone before. If we only have a nice, kind heart, that might help us to not attack ourselves, but we won't take the bold step of moving into the now, of being open and vulnerable to whatever beckons us into new territory.

When we go into new territory, we don't know what's going to happen. We might go crazy. We might die. We might fall into a black hole and never come out. So we think, "I'm always going to stay on this side of the event horizon. Who wants to go into a black hole? I might get absorbed. Or who knows where I might end up?"

Many of us now know that a black hole is the beginning of a wormhole. But it took a lot of research to discover that if you move into a black hole, it takes you to another place, another realm. So, we imagine that we're going to disappear. And who wants to disappear? "I'd rather stay in the realm of the event horizon and have some experiences . . ."

It takes an adventurous spirit to say, "Well, let's jump and see what happens." But remember that the jumping is not a matter of doing anything. It's more about the sense of courage, of boldness in that whatever arises, whatever happens, we will allow ourselves to be vulnerable to it.

So compassion is necessary, but it needs to be balanced with a strength in the form of an adventurous spirit, a spirit that wants to experience the unknown. We're talking about a sense of vitality and strength that is not passively waiting for things to happen, but is dynamic and interested in what might arise at any moment. We're talking about being ready to go—although we don't go anywhere, really. We just keep being where we are in every moment.

KEEPING THE BALANCE

Inner practice is not boot camp. Boldness doesn't mean pushing ourselves. It doesn't demand that we jam ourselves into a particular place. The balanced combination of strength and kindness that we have been describing shows us that what we want to develop over time in our practice is a kind of bold vulnerability in which we're kind *and* strong *and* courageous. Sometimes the kindness is more in the foreground. Sometimes the boldness is in the foreground. The boldness continues to be a courageous strength and adventurousness without becoming foolhardy, without becoming harsh. We're not pushing ourselves, saying, "Okay, you wimp, why don't you just move into this?" That's not what I mean by being courageous.

So that's when the kindness is important. Kindness has attunement, a recognition of exactly where we are. And if we have strength as well, we will naturally allow ourselves to be vulnerable, to be open to what's arising and allow ourselves to be there and in the moment—whatever it is.

When we blend courage and compassion, assertiveness and gentleness, our essential strength and kindness support us in being where we are. These qualities open us to be with our primary experience and keep us from being distracted by or concerned with the secondary reactions of our internal aggression. With them, we are infused with a bold vulnerability that leads us more and more into the immediacy and intimacy of being real.

EXPLORATION SESSION

Deepening the Inquiry

Now that you have some understanding of the primary and secondary components of experience, as well as the capacities that are needed to stay present with and explore your experience and some of the obstacles that may arise, let's do another exploration of your experience. Take fifteen minutes to do this inquiry. Without focusing on any capacities or obstacles, just be present in each moment, aware of what's happening and attuned to where you are in that process. Let whatever wants to arise manifest itself naturally, and follow it.

Notice when you are in touch with your primary experience and when you are more focused on a reaction or attitude toward the experience. Can you sense the difference? What happens when you are being with the primary experience?

You may be able to observe changes in your experience that reflect a deepening and expanding of where you are. After you have done this, consider your inquiry to see how the qualities of kindness and courage manifested. How and where did kindness show up? Did it have the quality of timidity? Where did courage or boldness manifest? Did it have an edge of harshness?

CHAPTER 7

Following Truth to
Meaning and Harmony

I HAVE BEEN ENCOURAGING YOU to become more aware of what you are experiencing and to understand what you are experiencing in order to know where you are. And I have indicated that knowing *where* you are will lead you to knowing and being the deeper nature of *what* you are. But it is useful to keep in mind that what you are is not separate from the deepest nature of reality itself. This true reality is a nondual oneness of pure Being.

However, many people find that when they are in touch with the transcendent nature of reality—the oneness of all things and beings—then who and where they are in the moment feels irrelevant or disappears into the oneness. Others have the experience that the True Nature of reality cares nothing for the more ordinary aspects of their life. And many spiritual paths take the point of view that our familiar personality, or ego, is only a barrier to what is true and real, and thus it needs to be transcended.

If we take the latter position, how do we make sense of this notion that knowing and understanding where we are in any given moment has a particular, revelatory relationship to our True Nature, which is also the True Nature of reality? In this chapter, we will explore this question of large and small truth—primordial and partial truth—and how the thread of understanding links the individuality of one's life with the nondual oneness of reality.

THE UNFOLDING JOURNEY TO TRUE NATURE

Let us start with the recognition that reality itself doesn't actually have levels. Reality—everything that exists—is all True Nature. It is all one thing. But because we go through stages in the unfoldment of discovering the truth—which is the truth of True Nature—it seems to us that reality has layers. Reality is sufficiently intelligent and vast to know that human beings recognize reality with different degrees of completeness. It knows that each degree of recognition has its own possibility of truth because it is still reality; it's just not reality in its completeness.

That doesn't mean that we can have truth only if we see it completely. At every level of truth, comprehension and meaningfulness exists. With every glimpse of even partial truth, what we are seeing is being touched by the primordial reality, by the primordial harmony, and by the primordial truth itself. This provides us with a sense of a path or an unfoldment, a flow of experience that makes being where we are, and inquiring into that, a meaningful practice.

So what does that tell us about how to approach our work? As we have seen, our practice of learning to be where we are is a matter of inquiring to find out what is happening, what the truth of a situation is. To ask, "Where am I?" means, "What is the truth of my experience?" And to ask, "What is the truth of my experience?" means, "I want to understand it in a way that is meaningful to my heart, that nourishes my heart and my soul; I don't just want an explanation." An explanation that is not felt can be exact without being meaning-ful, in which case, it doesn't nourish us.

As we work with our experience—inquiring and delving into it, being present with it—the presence and the awareness that pervades our experience reveals itself to be that underlying truth, or True Nature, that we have been seeking. And as our understanding unfolds, the harmony of the various elements of our experience is a felt harmony of connectedness. That experience is closer to the inherent, original, primordial harmony that reveals—and actually is—the oneness of all things.

We could describe the path toward realization in this way: Our desire to understand where we are and who we are takes us on an initial journey of learning to have more and more insight about our ordinary experience. Gradually, we come to recognize the rela-tionship of ordinary experience to deeper levels of reality—how it reflects True Nature. Eventually, we are able to see how our individ-ual experience is nothing but True Nature, and we move toward the realization of pure Being—the oneness that is nondual reality.

This recognition of the nondual ground of experience is the real-ization that there is basically only presence. Presence is what exists, what is, and everything that exists is a form that presence takes. Real-ity is one unified field of luminosity that differentiates itself into the various perceptions that we have. Thus, True Nature and Being are really the same thing as truth, or reality. All those terms mean the same thing: presence that is in a condition of conscious full realiza-tion. In this condition, experience is not filtered through the mind; things are experienced exactly as they are. We see their nature and recognize that it is True Nature—which turns out to be the nature of everything, all the way down to the tiniest particle.

This means that nothing exists but True Nature. It pervades everything so intimately, so completely, that it doesn't leave any one spot unoccupied by it.

GOT MEANING?

This recognition that only True Nature exists is expressed in differ-ent ways by various spiritual cultures and traditions. A Vedantist would say, "I am That," because what is real is referred to as "That." A Buddhist would call it the suchness of reality. A Taoist says, "The real Tao is beyond words and names." A Christian mystic will say, "God is the unknowable transcendent unity of all." All of these dif-ferent approaches basically attempt to refer to reality in a way that takes it away from the mind and the idea that mind can define it. It is what it is. It is the truth independent of mind, more specifically, of discursive mind.

As we move toward the West, to the Sufi tradition, we find that the word Sufis use for True Nature translates into something close to the word "meaning." They also call it "truth," but when Sufis are referring to the essential presence, the essential nature—that which underlies everything—it is *meaning* that they want to emphasize.

This is one reason why I think of Sufism as a Western tradition. Many people associate Sufism with the East because they know Sufis from India. But Sufism came out of the Middle East, which, along with Greece, is the birthplace of Western thought. Thus, the origins of Sufi thought are rooted in Greek and Middle Eastern soils.

What makes Sufism more of a Western than an Eastern tradition is the fact that it relates True Nature to the mind and calls it "mean-ing." But what Sufis are pointing to is not what we usually call mean-ing. Their word for "meaning"—*ma'na*—signifies that which is substantial, important, what matters. It is the meaning to the soul, the meaning to the heart, not to the mind as we conceive of mind today. That is because in general the Sufis say that the organ of true knowing is the heart. So this sense that True Nature is true knowing or meaning is in contrast to the traditions of the East, in which the emphasis is *beyond* knowing.

I am focusing on the word "meaning" because I think it will help us better understand what it means to be where we are. In the condition of realization, the meaning we are experiencing is not the conceptual meaning; it is the very presence of reality. When we experience it, it is the meaning of existence. It is meaningful to the soul and to the heart. Or we could say: The soul and the heart feel that existence is meaningful. Existence got meaning. What's the meaning it got? True Nature.

DISCOVERING A
SEAMLESS HARMONY

Thus, in this condition of nondual realization, one perceives a transparency and a luminosity of oneness and at the same time a seamless harmony in the manifestations of that oneness. Whatever the situation, what we would normally distinguish as bad or good is experienced as a seamless and graceful harmony that is simple but beautiful, aesthetically inspiring and uplifting. What's more, the harmony between everything is also meaningful; it is part of the meaning. So, the meaning is the presence itself; it is the totality of reality in its harmony.

We begin the inner work of exploring our experience from a point that is far from that recognition of harmony. Before we take on the work of inquiry, life seems empty and meaningless, and we feel dissatisfied and discontented. We look for significance, for meaning, for an inherent value to our life that we don't recognize yet. As we come to understand what is happening in our experience, we see some truth and some meaning, but it is not yet the final meaning. It does, however, have a flavor of truth in that the understanding itself brings a harmony that reflects the inherent harmony of the universe and of truth itself.

Even in the initial stages of our work, as we get insight into what is happening in our experience, the truth that we see is meaningful in some way. At this first stage, that meaningfulness reveals a harmony, an interconnection between the various elements in our experience that we didn't see before. So meaning, which is based on making connections, is felt as a growing harmony based on the truth in our experience. And that truth reflects the True Nature that is the essence of the harmony, that makes harmony possible.

So, for example, I might have been dealing with the issue of being weak and thinking, "I haven't got any strength. I can't say no; I can't be myself." At the first level, I might come to understand that this lack of strength to stand up for myself is related to not feeling my own identity as truly separate from others in my life. Understanding how this is part of my personal history brings a certain harmony to my experience based on recognizing a personal truth.

At a later point in the inner journey, it becomes more obvious that this harmony or understanding is connected to essential presence. At this next stage, the strength essence arises and I feel strong, able to be a separate person who feels free to say no. It all fits together, because the arising of the essential quality itself answers all the questions about separation, self-assertion, and autonomy, and also reveals the inherent harmony.

In other words, at the second stage, I am feeling the sense of strength because I can see that these manifestations of clarity, expansion, energy, and capacity are related to feeling separate, and I didn't know that before. Now, as I understand my issue of separation—with my husband, or my wife, or my children, or my mother—the presence arises and I feel the true separation in which I am separate from my mind in the sense that I do not need any ideas or beliefs to be myself. Everything I have been experiencing is now meaningful. It all makes sense, all of it fits, and I am seeing the truth. The truth I am aware of now *is* the meaning, and the center of that meaning is the essential presence itself.

At the third and most conscious stage of the journey, I recognize that meaning as being implicit in everything. The meaning is essential presence, which is revealed as the nature of everything—the nondual reality of True Nature. So the meaning and the harmony are actually inseparable at this point in the journey.

So, to summarize:

- In the first stage, the harmony becomes apparent as the understanding of your experience reveals the meaning of that experience. You feel more like yourself, more real, as you understand the situation and see the truth.
- In the second stage you begin to recognize what makes you real and where the truth comes from. When you recognize the essential presence itself, you see that the source of realness, truth, meaning, and harmony is all True Nature because it is absolute authenticity—it is undefiled, incorruptible realness.
- In the third stage, presence reveals itself as the nature and meaning of everything, and you experience life as the harmonious differentiations of that presence.

HARMONY AS INTERRELATEDNESS

Understanding relates directly to discerning the harmony in the situation that is implicit but not clear to us yet. And because we are in a limited place of realization, we can only see the harmony by seeing interconnectedness, how things relate to each other. As we see the meaningfulness of those connections, we begin to sense the harmony. "Oh, I was feeling scared yesterday after my work with my teacher, and today I am feeling empty . . . now as I pay attention, I can recognize my projection onto my teacher . . . which reminds me of this incident with my mother . . ." We can relate these together as if they were somehow connected at some point, because we are beginning to discern an underlying harmony. And that happens as we relate one impression to another.

We saw earlier that the ultimate harmony in the condition of nondual realization is the recognition that the harmony is nothing but the seamless connectedness of everything that is. You are able to recognize that everything is manifesting the same reality. And you can also observe that it manifests itself so that nothing clouds anything else, nothing obscures or displaces anything else—everything melds together in a graceful harmony. This graceful harmony is the basis of all the laws, or order, of nature. So part of learning how to understand our experience is in finding the order that is in it. This happens when we can interrelate one component with another.

To take another example: As you are exploring your experience, components both in the present moment and from the past are aris-ing. You experienced something in your inquiry with your teacher yesterday that is the same or similar to something you experienced a week ago at work . . . and that is interconnected with an experience ten years previously in another job . . . and that is connected with something that happened fifty years ago with your father. When all of this becomes interconnected in your understanding, it can bring more of a sense of a harmony to your experience now.

INTERRELATING THROUGH
CONTRASTING AND COMPARING

A key part of the process of understanding in inquiry involves uncov-ering relationships between things. To do that, you have to place them next to each other to see how they are related. You need to compare and contrast them: how are they the same or different, and if they are different, in what way are they different? In this process of interrelating by contrasting, a constant comparison is happening. You are comparing your experience yesterday with your teacher to your experience a week ago in your job, to your experience ten years ago in a previous job, to your experience fifty years ago with your father. Through contrast and comparison, at some point you arrive at a sense of what the similarity among them is or what they are all pointing to that is common to each experience.

You can see from this that it is inherent in our discrimination, in our capacity to know, that we contrast, interrelate, and compare things. I might say, "Yesterday I was really terrified, and today I am just scared, so I can say that I was much more scared yesterday. And, a week ago with my teacher I was anxious, but I can see that anxiety is really related to that terror, and with my father I was really afraid."

So, not only can we compare, but we can also make objective

assessments or judgments—the way a scientist would in comparing data from an experiment. We can make determinations such as, this is greater than that, that is smaller than this, this is more scary than that, this is more alive than that, that is more intense than this, and so on. All of this comparison is necessary for our understanding.

Even when we are not in the process of inquiry, we understand what is happening in our daily life because our mind is always corre-lating, contrasting, and judging. Without this, there is no knowledge and certainly no scientific knowledge. What we see here is that com-parative judgment is an important part of discerning the truth. And comparative judgment, in the scientific sense, always leads to the recognition of the meaning and implications that result from the comparisons that are made. This means that to understand your cur-rent patterns, you also have to understand their relationship to what happened in your past.

In our example, you would need to recognize that fifty years ago, when you were a child with your father, you were too little to stand up for yourself. Now you are an adult—bigger, stronger—and you see things differently. You need to have the ability to judge—to see that particular truth and to recognize its meaning and implications. That is what is called a scientific assessment or a scientific judgment of the situation. "I can now see that when I was only eleven, I couldn't stand up for myself with my dad, but now I am sixty-one, so, accord-ing to my assessment, I have more capacity to take care of myself and to be my authentic self."

In this way, the process of inquiry moves on in a continuum of correlation, contrast, comparison, assessment, and judgment—but all of it is neutral. If you are looking at your experience scientifically, when you say, "Yesterday I was more terrified than I am today," you are not saying which is better. You have no sense that you would rather feel less terrified today or that you should. Your statement is only for the sake of understanding that you were more terrified yes-terday than you are today.

That's because if you see that you were more terrified yesterday and recognize what caused that to be so, you might discover the factors that make the terror be more or less present. If you don't see that contrast, if you don't make that comparative judgment, you won't be able to get to the insight that the terror really had to do with emptiness, because you were also feeling more empty yesterday than you are today.

MOVING FROM COMPARATIVE TO MORAL JUDGMENT

However, the mind, because of our desire, because of our insecurity, because of our deprivation, takes the judgment a step further. Since the mind is defined by the ego and its inherent ignorance, it says, "I don't want to feel this the way I felt it yesterday." If I were observing rats in an experiment, and I saw that one of them was more terrified today than it had been on some other day, I could easily keep a neutral position about that. But now I'm talking about myself, so it becomes personal. My judgment is affected by the familiar sense of being a separate individual. Not only have I made an assessment or judgment, but a preference for one condition over another has entered in—a desire for it to be this way and not that way.

That is how comparative judgment, which inherently is a neutral function in our investigations, can become moral judgment. We hold it that one condition is better, more desirable, than another. And not only that—we also think that the condition or feeling we prefer is what we should go after. Comparative judgment thus becomes one of the primary barriers against being where we actually are.

Our mind naturally compares whatever we experience with other feelings and other experiences—both our own and those of other people. Perhaps you're meditating and you start feeling a little bubbling in your belly, something you haven't experienced before. A neutral response says, "That's interesting, in contrast to yesterday when there was no bubbling." However, it is more likely that when you feel the bubbling, you remember your friend who said that when he was meditating the other day, he had this lava flow—intense heat and brightness and a tremendous explosion. And you think, "All I feel is this little bubble? This is all I got? Obviously, what's happening for me is not *it*."

Or maybe it changes from a bubble into a big, exploding supernova, and you remember your friend talking about the lava, and you think, "What happened to him is nothing—*this* is it!" You want to hold on to the experience until you talk to him . . . whose is bigger? That sounds really funny, but it happens all the time. We don't leave our experience alone. The problem is not the fact that we compare, but that we compare in a judgmental way. Our superego dominates our observations and we end up saying, "This is acceptable, that is not acceptable." Everything is seen as good or bad, preferable or not, more evolved than someone else's experience or not, and the result is that we can't let ourselves be where we are.

Our tendency usually is not to uncover the pure scientific insight, the truth. Our orientation is to get something out of our experience because we are driven by our desires and our emptiness and our insecurities and so on. We evaluate whether our experience is better or worse, instead of simply recognizing, neutrally, that it is different from what it was before. We lose sight of the fact that if we can recognize the difference as it is, that will help us get the insight we need to really understand it. We meddle with it—pushing it, pulling it, resisting it, defending against it, trying to hold on to it—to make it be what we think is better.

And that doesn't only happen when you are comparing yourself to your friends. Maybe you've read a great treatise by an ancient sage who describes enlightenment, and you are trying to duplicate or imitate his ideals of spiritual practice. You are constantly meditating and are practically enlightened, but every time you experience something, you feel, "No, that's not it . . . it doesn't measure up." You always judge what is happening in your meditations against the standard of the teaching. But you could compare it in a scientific sense: "The teacher says this, and I am feeling another way. Let me see what that is, if it is not what he seems to be talking about."

Using the scientific method of observation and exploration, we arrive at a clearer understanding that could actually move us closer to what the teacher is saying. But if we say, "No, that is not it; what I'm experiencing is no good," we become disappointed, dejected, depressed. On the other hand, if we think things are going well, we can get proud of ourselves and grandiose, with our nose up in the air, such that nobody can even speak to us in a reasonable way.

RECOGNIZING OUR EXPERIENCE AS A GIFT

Since we are always measuring and making moral judgments about our situation, it is difficult for us to recognize that our experience now is what we have been given: "What I am experiencing now is the only thing that the universe is giving me, and in fact, it fits me one hundred percent. If I really take it on and begin to understand it, it contains everything I need to know about myself." Because the experience you are experiencing now is all about you: whatever's in it that you think is good, whatever you think is bad—everything that is about you is in it. Having your friend's experience might be nifty for a while, but it doesn't nourish you much because it isn't telling you about you.

So when comparative judgment becomes dominated by the superego, you are missing the capacity to appreciate your experience in the now. You are cut off from recognizing that it is precious, and you cannot see that this is the gift you are being given right now to understand yourself. You don't recognize that it is the reflection of the harmony that is the true primordial harmony. So you try to push it in a different direction.

As you can see, comparative judgment becomes implicit in our ego operation every time we try to live according to an ideal. If we are always measuring ourselves against an ego ideal—whether it's success or intelligence or a spiritual ideal of love or maturity or enlightenment—then we are not being where we are. We decide that where we are is not okay. It's as though you were always being told to go to your room. Every time your experience arises, somebody is telling you, "Go to your room—I don't want to see you; I don't want to hear you." Imagine people telling you that. If every time you show up that happens, you won't want to show up again.

You could approach it like this: "I can allow myself to see how this harmony is trying to present itself in my situation right now. If I respect my experience and let it be, if I make myself available to discover its truth, it will unfold to reveal the harmony that is relevant for me, that is destined for me."

It's important to realize that just about anything can become an ideal, a standard: our own past experience, another person's experience, our teacher's state, a precept taught in a book—whatever we come across on our path. Any of these things can be useful for comparison and to help us understand our situation, but that is not the same thing as always measuring ourselves in comparison to them in a judgmental, negative way, in a manner that is violent toward our experience.

When you consider what we have said thus far, you might get the idea that you have to stop yourself from judging. But I am not saying, "Don't judge." Because if we try to stop ourselves from feeling judgment, we won't be able to see the judgment that is there. What is left for us to do instead is to continue our practice. If judgment arises, we include it in our awareness. When we do not suppress judgment, and we see it for what it is, we are freed from it—without trying to get free.

Our awareness is big enough to hold judgment too, so if you are willing to look at judgment and understand it as something else that is arising in your experience, you won't struggle against it. Struggling against it is just another way of meddling, of saying, "My experience shouldn't include this." It is another form of rejection, of not being where you are.

So, now we have seen how a neutral process that helps us discern truth can be twisted into an impediment to seeing the truth. Being where we are means being with whatever happens to be arising, without preference or judgment. In every situation and condition, we can be interested in our experience, we can open to it and let ourselves just be there. This invites the revelation of interconnectedness and meaning—and ultimately the implicit harmony in the reality we are living. In this way, we can open to what the universe is giving us at this very moment.

EXPLORATION SESSION

Discovering How Comparative Judgment Operates in You

Take some time to sit with your experience as it arises moment to moment and observe how your mind responds as things come and go. Notice when comparative judgment operates in an effective, functional way. How does that lead you to see the truth of your experience?

Notice when you shift from a neutral observation into taking a moral position about any feeling, thought, or desire that arises. What happens to your sense of being present with your experience? What makes it possible to shift back into neutral and simply be with what is arising without judging it? Are there particular areas of your experience about which you tend to be more judgmental?

CHAPTER 8

Finding True Acceptance

WE HAVE SEEN IN THE LAST chapter that when our capacity for discernment, as it manifests in comparative assessment or judgment, becomes usurped by the needs or desires of the ego, it becomes a deadly thing. It becomes deadly for our being, for our capacity to be real, to be ourselves, because it makes it impossible for us to be where we are.

When we engage in that kind of comparative judgment, the next step is that we say no to our experience. We compare whatever is arising in our field to something else, and we want to replace it with something we think is better. And that means that whatever is arising in our experience is not what we want. It is as though God had sent us a gift, and we send it back marked "Wrong address."

Usually, we're not aware of the divisiveness of that inner activity. Whenever we say, "I don't want that" or "That's not it" about our experience, we are talking about something that is arising that is part of us. Yet we want to take it and throw it in the garbage: "It should be disposed of. I should have something else. Otherwise, I won't be satisfied. For me to hold and embrace what is there, it has to be what I think is supposed to be there, what I think is best, what I think is preferable, what I think is ideal, what I think I'm looking for."

In other words, if you go past neutral, objective, comparative judgment and move into moralistic, comparative judgment, you're not only saying, "That's not it," you're saying, "Get out." You're not only measuring everything in your experience from the perspective of trying to attain a particular state, result, or goal—and judging it from that standard—you're creating the ground for rejecting your own experience.

So, your comparison is not just a measurement against something else, it's a measurement that includes a pushing away. That's the bias. And how can you be where you are if you are rejecting something important that is happening where you are? Whatever is happening, that is how your experience is emerging. If you are rejecting your experience, how are you going to be there?

In contrast, the objective kind of measurement or comparative judgment does not involve idealization. It simply looks at an experience and says, "Okay, this is different than it was yesterday" or "It's different from what this other person is experiencing," but there is no pushing. You aren't doing anything to your experience. And because you can recognize how it is different, you can allow it to be as it is; you have the space to hold it. As a result, it is possible to be where you are.

REJECTION OF OUR EXPERIENCE
IS SELF-REJECTION

The deadly thing about comparative moral judgment is that it leads to the rejection of our experience. What's even more significant is that the rejection of experience is inherently a self-rejection— because our experience is part of us. Remember, all of our experiences are nothing but forms within our own consciousness. They're all arising out of the same awareness—the same beingness manifesting itself in various forms. Here it appears as a little bubbling; there it could seem like a volcanic eruption. But whether it's a volcanic eruption, a little bubbling, or a raging sun, it is just our soul manifesting in that possibility. When we say no to it, when we want to throw it away, we are actually saying no to ourselves. We're saying no to our consciousness, to our awareness. We're saying, "This consciousness is not doing its thing correctly. Let's get rid of it."

So, the rejection of anything that is arising in our consciousness automatically becomes a self-rejection. How are we going to be ourselves if we're rejecting ourselves? How are we going to be present with ourselves? Imagine somebody rejecting you—is it easy to be there? How do you feel when you feel rejected? Is it a little thing? You might say, "Oh, a person's rejecting me—not a big deal."

But being rejected is a big deal for human beings. Being rejected goes further than someone saying, "You're not it." That in itself is difficult to tolerate, but rejection is someone saying, "I don't want you. I'm done with you." Because of this we're always busy making sure we don't get rejected.

You can probably recall a time when you were getting ready for a first date. Remember how terrible the anxiety was as you spent all that time trying to find a sexier hairstyle, or put together just the right thing to wear, or whatever else you thought you needed to do to show up looking okay. Why? So you wouldn't be rejected. You didn't even need to be loved, you just didn't want to be rejected.

Almost everyone is continually dealing with rejection in some form. Most people constantly reject their emotions: "I'm feeling anger now . . . I shouldn't feel anger. I'm feeling weak . . . oh, that's terrible. I'm feeling love . . . I definitely can't feel *that*; that person's married!" Whatever's arising that we think we don't want, we reject it—we don't want to experience it. And we want to be casual about it, too; we'd like to deal with those feelings as though we were sweeping dirt off a floor. But what we think of as the dirt is us. That's because nothing exists outside of our experience, our own consciousness. Your experience is not like the contents of a purse that you can throw away. Experience is the actual fabric of the purse—so if you try to throw part of your experience away, you are tearing yourself apart.

The more you reject something in yourself, the more you tear yourself apart—because that something is *you*. It doesn't matter what it is—hatred, or frustration, or love, or grandiosity, or anything else; if you're trying to push it away, sweep it away, get rid of it, what results is a tremendous tearing apart of the soul. It affects you that way even though you don't know it.

Rejection is remarkably painful in a way that is not easily understood. Do we know why we try so hard to avoid it? We know that being rejected by someone is humiliating. It is belittling. It's diminishing. People feel distraught or destroyed when they feel rejected. Why is that? Why is the experience of rejection such a devastating thing?

The first rejection most people were engaged in occurred in infancy, when they threw up milk. Even if you can't remember that far back, you've probably had several experiences of throwing up something you ate or drank. The prototype of rejection is throwing something up. Something you've taken in doesn't taste good—it doesn't feel right—so you throw it up. That is rejection.

What's the experience like of throwing something up? How are you feeling as you do that? Throwing up is not a neutral, easygoing activity. It's not like a polite request: "Please leave the room now." When you throw up, your whole body convulses. It is instinctual and violent. Rejection has within it this intense desire to get rid of something that seems horrible—a kind of revulsion: "Yuck! Don't bring it near me! Get rid of it!"

Now imagine that somebody is directing that kind of intense, violent, repulsive energy at you. It is humiliating. That's why it hurts. That's why it's so devastating. That's why we try to run away from it.

The attitude of rejection is something we need to understand. It's not just a mental orientation. When the soul is saying no and denying a part of itself, the attitude of rejection is a reflection of the same kind of violent reaction that causes us to throw something up.

Because we know how much we dislike something when we vomit it up, we can appreciate that we unconsciously fear such a violent reaction being aimed at us, and we avoid rejection internally (from our superego) as well as externally (from others).

When we reject something in our experience, that's what we're doing—we're trying to throw out part of ourselves. We're not just getting rid of it by taking it out and throwing it away; we are trying to throw it away with an emotionally violent action similar to vomiting it out. You want to vomit up yourself, or part of yourself. It's that devastating. So, that's really what's deadly about comparative moral judgment. It becomes the ground upon which we want to divest ourselves of something, and the way we do that damages our soul. Rejection, disapproval, or looking down on something that we think doesn't measure up are not just detached positions we take about our experience; they are violent, destructive behaviors we use to harm ourselves.

How does our soul react to this aggressive wounding attitude? In the same way you would react if you thought someone you were about to meet for a first date was going to reject you. What would you do? First, you'd get anxious. And if the anxiety got severe enough, you might chicken out. Your date arrives, is waiting for you, and you don't show up. Or maybe you call at the last minute and make an excuse: "I'm sorry, I can't make it tonight . . . maybe next week."

When a friend later asks you why, you say, "I don't know; I guess I was too scared."

And your friend says, "What were you scared of? What did you think was going to happen? The worst that could happen is that she'd reject you."

And your response is, "What do you mean, 'that's the worst . . .'?!"

If we have a tendency to reject our experience, a part of us is going to feel the same as the person in this example: "I'm not going to show myself. I'm going to hide or cover myself up or pretend I'm like this or that I'm not like that." After a while, if we keep doing this, we're not aware anymore of what's going on inside us. That awareness is not even possible for us because parts of our experience are so suppressed that they don't even come up to be seen. Or, if they do arise, they're so camouflaged or defended that we can't become aware of what they really are. If we can't be aware, we can't understand. If we can't understand, we can't be fully there. If we can't be there, present, we can't be ourselves. If we can't be ourselves, we can't be real.

We can't be real if we reject ourselves. It's as simple as that. It doesn't matter what comes up; we can't reject anything that arises in ourselves and be real.

Saints are not people who have no terrible thoughts. They can have the worst thoughts in the world. They just don't do anything about them; they don't put them into action. Imagine a saint having a bad thought and saying, "Yuck!" What kind of saint is that? But that's how we think saints are. And we think they'll disapprove of us if we have a bad thought or do something harmful.

So, what can we do instead of rejecting our experience? Of course, the first thing is not to reject our rejection. Remember the regression that you can get into if you are not aware: "Uh-oh, this is rejection again—terrible, horrible! Look at me. I'm rejecting my experience. I'm supposed to be allowing and spacious and spiritual, but I'm not. Isn't that humiliating?" The practice is to be aware of the rejection, to hold it, to recognize it, to let it transform to its true quality, as we discussed in chapter 2.

Of course, the experience of rejection has many implications that we need to be aware of. These issues concern the ways we were rejected, who rejected us, and how we internalized the rejection. We may notice certain patterns of how we experience ourselves when we feel rejected and whether we identify more with the one who is rejecting or the one who is rejected. The more we study our experience—what arises in our consciousness—the more we will see the activity of rejection, ranging from quite gross condemnation to very subtle dismissal.

ACCEPTANCE AS RESIGNATION

You might be thinking at this point that the best alternative to rejecting your experience is to do the opposite. What is the opposite of rejection? Acceptance. You see what's arising—you see your weakness or your hatred or your vulnerability—and now you don't reject it, you just accept it. But we need to look closer at this to uncover what may be underneath it.

For most people, acceptance means, "What's there is there. I might as well accept it since I can't do anything about it." But that implies, "I still don't like it, but I can't change it so I just have to accept it." That kind of acceptance may seem to be the opposite of rejection, but it actually has rejection embedded in it. It means, "I'm just trying to do the right thing. Inside, I really am rejecting this experience, but I want to be a good practitioner, so I'm going to act as if I accept it."

True acceptance doesn't contain any kind of attitude of rejection. It is not a humiliating, violent throwing up, nor does it bring up any repulsion in the soul. It's just there. Something arises, and you don't respond with a moral or preferential invested judgment. You just recognize the feeling or experience for what it is, whether it's something that feels good or doesn't feel good. You experience it with presence and awareness. Your sense of satisfaction or contentment doesn't depend on whether it meets a particular standard that you have set up for your experience.

So, when I say that rejection doesn't work, that it's an impediment to our practice, this doesn't mean that the antidote—or what people call the antidote—is to accept it. Because that "antidote" has within in it an implicit rejection, as well as a judgmental attitude. And why is that? Because to accept instead of reject is really saying: "It's better not to reject, so I'll accept, which means I'm not going to push it away; I'm going to resign myself to it."

ACCEPTANCE AS GRASPING

But we also commonly experience a form of acceptance that is not resignation. This happens when we like our experience. We think we are accepting, when what we are actually doing is grasping at or holding on to an experience that we like having.

What happens when we judge our experience to be good or desirable? We say we accept it, and we can then say that acceptance is the opposite of rejection. But what does that really mean in this case? We generally do not reject the experiences and feelings that feel good. But is that true acceptance?

Let's say I'm feeling really holy right now. Or I just had a humble feeling. Maybe I remember that I did something generous a little while ago, so I'm having a warm, loving feeling about myself. Of course, I'm not going to reject any of those feelings. What I have here is an attached acceptance. I *want* to feel that way about myself. I'm invested in it. Most likely, I'm judging it as better than the time I was selfish or arrogant or whatever I consider to be unholy, impure. So, instead of pushing away my experience, I'm holding on to it. I want to keep it for myself; I don't want it to go away.

TRUE ACCEPTANCE

It is very rare for people to know true acceptance. That's partly because the word "acceptance" usually is seen as being the opposite of rejection—if I'm not rejecting something, I must be accepting it. Rejection pushes away. Acceptance takes in, whether in a resigned or a grasping way. If I don't throw something out, I munch on it and eat it up instead. I either push away or take in—either reject or accept—these are the two ways we usually relate to our experience.

The acceptance of True Nature is quite a different thing. True acceptance does not grasp or hold on to anything. It says, "I'm happy being myself—it's irrelevant whether what I'm eating right now is good food or bad food. I'm fine with it. I can be here with it. It's interesting. It may taste terrible or it may taste delicious. I'm open to the situation." In this case, there is no need to judge it one way or another.

If I truly accept my experience—without comparative moral judgment about it—then I am not disappointed about it. Neither am I happy about it. I'm neither satisfied nor dissatisfied. I don't need to feel anything in particular about it. I'm just fine with it the way it is.

So, most of the time, when people think they are in acceptance, they are either wanting to hold on to something they feel good about or they have become resigned to something that they don't feel good about, because they don't know what else to do.

The latter often happens when people struggle with something in the physical realm. Perhaps somebody says, "I've finally accepted my weight." What does acceptance mean in this case? Most of the time it means, "I've tried and tried to lose weight, but it's never really worked. I'd rather not have it that way. If I could, I'd change it. I'd cut away some of this fat. But now I'm not bothering to do anything more about it." That's not true acceptance. That is resignation.

True acceptance isn't a judgment that my weight should be different from what it is. True acceptance says, "Since this is how it is, I'm interested in experiencing it and fully being with it; I am totally present and I'm being here with energy, with interest, with enthusiasm about life." The resigned kind of acceptance diminishes enthusiasm. It's not an attitude of True Nature—it's an ego attitude that is actually deflated rejection, a rejection without aliveness. Likewise, the grasping acceptance, which is a sticky kind of attachment, is not true acceptance either.

What we call true acceptance is more of a contented awareness—an awareness that's content with itself. It's not busy judging and rejecting what's arising in it. True acceptance is not invested. It is not attached to any desire or need for things to be different from how they are.

Over time and with practice, we become more skilled at seeing, recognizing, and understanding these reactions to our experience—the rejection, the resigned acceptance, and the grasping acceptance. This makes us more and more able to be with our experience as it is.

That's why we say that our practice is just presence with aware-ness. Presence with awareness doesn't reject, but it doesn't grasp either. When we are simply present and aware in our experiencing, we can begin to recognize the true condition that is arising. We notice our inner attitude becoming simpler and more subtle as we are being with our experience.

We begin to feel an openness, a vulnerability, an allowing that has a sense of subtle contentment and satisfaction. The fact that our presence is arising in this way reveals the experience to be an expres-sion of our True Nature. This quality in our consciousness does not arise because something specific is happening that is to our liking. True acceptance arises on its own as a result of our being present with our reactions—our tendencies to reject or grasp—without being run by them.

It is this kind of acceptance that is necessary for us to handle the peach correctly. Do you remember the peach that we talked about in chapter 3? The peach is no good, so you put it away, but you don't reject your feeling. You don't reject the taste. It doesn't matter what the taste is like. It could be rotten or sweet. You take note of the sen-sations of taste, but being yourself—being who you are—doesn't change; your inner balance remains. You do not engage in any push-ing or pulling that will divide you.

Rejection divides the soul within itself. It says, "I am here, and I am rejecting this experience in me and making it into something other than me." That's what rejection is: making something in us be an "other" that is not part of us.

So we can see more clearly now from these examples that when re-jection accompanies comparative moral judgment, judgment loses its scientific neutrality and becomes based in the ego. Scientific neutral-ity means engaging in comparative judgment without having a pref-erential attitude. With that balanced neutrality, which is a kind of serenity, we remain alive, aware, and conscious, because we're inves-tigating, we're interested. Our attitude is open and allowing with a contentment in seeking the truth. And that brings us back to the foundation of all of our exploration in the work that we are doing:

Whatever our experience is, we are interested in being present with it and finding out the truth about it. Learning not to reject or get attached to whatever arises will help us do that as fully as possible.

EXPLORATION SESSION

Discerning True Acceptance of Your Experience

This exercise will help you to explore how acceptance and rejection function in your experience. In this session, you will be following your moment-to-moment process in present time.

The aim is to be where you are—whatever you are experiencing—and follow your experience as it unfolds for at least fifteen minutes. You are not trying to have a particular experience of acceptance. You can see things, compare them, and understand them, but you don't need to do anything at all about them. You are simply experiencing.

After you have finished, go back and review what happened. As you remember your experience, notice when and how the different elements arose. Was rejection active? When did you experience resigned acceptance? When did grasping acceptance show up? What kinds of thoughts, feelings, and perceptions led to the experience of rejection?

Did you shift into true acceptance at certain points? How did that happen? Which element did you find yourself most often engaged in? What kinds of patterns do you observe about your process in the area of acceptance and rejection?

CHAPTER 9

Hatred and the
Power to Be

W E ARE BEGINNING TO SEE more clearly now that the practice of being oneself—finding where we are and simply abiding there—expresses our True Nature because our nature inherently doesn't do anything to itself. True Nature manifests everything, but in its purity, it is totally settled, unruffled, undivided—it is complete stillness and peace. If we don't engage in trying to change ourselves and instead allow ourselves to be where we are, where we are will spontaneously manifest this True Nature in our experience. However, as we have seen, the inner activities that we engage in to alter our experience are often what stop our True Nature from manifesting. Most of what we work with in our practice in some way addresses the various manifestations of this continual attempt to change ourselves.

All this inner activity makes it difficult for us to be ourselves in two fundamental ways. First, our interference blocks the arising of who we truly are. Because we do not embrace whatever is arising, our experience doesn't have a chance to unfold and manifest True Nature. Our activity prevents it from expressing its natural dynamism, its natural tendency to simply and spontaneously self-reveal, and so we do not perceive or recognize our True Nature.

Second, when we think that practice means changing our inner condition instead of letting it change itself, we are taking an orientation toward ourselves that is inherently very different from that of our True Nature. In other words, by siding with this inner activity, we disconnect from our True Nature. Our True Nature is simply thereness. So, by being internally active, we dissociate, we become something different than what we are, we leave our place of abiding. In some sense, we abandon our self, our nature, to become this active entity that is always trying to change itself.

And so we don't allow our experience to reveal its nature. That's because we take the view that there is something to accomplish. We think, "Realization is a result dependent on a cause, and that cause is my own effort. If I do such and such, this result will happen."

But that contradicts the reality that realization is what you already are, that you cannot accomplish yourself, you cannot go after yourself. You cannot change what is happening now so that you become yourself. You are already yourself; you just need to relax into it. When that happens, you recognize your True Nature.

THE TRAP OF INNER ACTIVITY

We have seen that this inner activity, which is the primary obstacle to being our True Nature, has many manifestations, which are various forms of resistance, control, and defensiveness. And we have also looked at various behaviors that are aimed specifically at changing our experience—attempts to conform to an ideal—rather than just letting ourselves be. All these behaviors imply self-rejection. All of them work against the natural revelation of our True Nature in all its luminosity.

We have also seen how inner and outer activity are related. Remember the peach? When you discover that it is rotten, you can either just put it away or you can put it away with a lot of internal activity going on. You may already recognize from your own experience that whenever we engage in an external activity, an inner activity usually goes along with it. Even when we are just sitting, continuous activity is almost always going on. We experience this mostly as incessant thinking, planning, trying to figure things out. But what we are doing is more fundamental than just being immersed in thoughts; we are in an energetic movement in which the dynamism of Being becomes contracted and dissociated. There is hesitation and a kind of inner stuttering. This inner busyness is what we mean by ego activity—an inner activity with a mental flavor and an agitated energetic quality. It lacks the smooth, spontaneous, effortless flow that is the manifestation of Being.

IDENTIFYING THE POWER
BEHIND OBSESSIVE ACTIVITY

Let's go a step further, now, and observe what is at work when this kind of activity intensifies and becomes habitual. You may have observed, for example, that when you are feeling insecure, when your desire to reach a particular state or outcome intensifies, or when you challenge the inner activity directly, the activity begins to take on a feverish quality. It can become quite rapid, incessant, even obsessive. You may even feel that you can't stop it—it is an energy that runs on its own, always thinking, doing, planning. This can occur as you engage in various efforts to get to a place other than where you actually are, including:

- Making explicit, repeated attempts to improve yourself in a particular area of your outer life
- Pushing yourself to create or maintain a specific inner state that you have hypothesized as desirable
- Striving to be different according to an ideal, an idea, a memory, a comparison with others, or a spiritual instruction
- Struggling to stop a particular feeling or thought from arising

- Experiencing continuous, rapid, agitated thinking, planning, and emotional activity around a particular topic or person
- Being driven toward a specific goal with increasing effort applied to achieve it
- Feeling constant dissatisfaction with yourself and a sense of failure or insufficiency

When one or more of these patterns begins to dominate your experience, it becomes possible to recognize something very important that you may not have seen before—something that can transform your inner state: the intensity of the experience itself can begin to expose the central energy that powers this obsessive, driven inner activity.

We have seen that the most effective motivation for our practice is kindness, which is compassionate in the sense that it is helpful, but which also has a quality of appreciativeness, a lovingness that reflects the energy of True Nature as it manifests its possibilities. We can see that the natural flow of our experience is fueled by love. In contrast, ego activity—especially when it gets obsessive—reveals an energy powering it that is very different in nature. If we observe carefully, we discover that the incessant, obsessive attempt to change ourselves, to improve ourselves, to be something different, is actually powered by self-hatred.

This may be difficult or painful to consider, but think about how much we criticize ourselves, judge ourselves, attack ourselves, reject ourselves, push and pull ourselves. What is behind it? Why would we want to be so violent toward ourselves?

If we keep examining our behavior, we will recognize at some point that what we are doing constantly in our inner activity is a form of violence. We may call it the activity of the superego or use some other term to describe it, but it is violence just the same. We can tell that it is violent because it hurts, it divides us inside, and it is constantly attacking the very nature of who we are.

The more we see the violence, the more we come to realize that it won't stop until we are willing to recognize a particular truth that most of the time we don't want to see. Some of us are aware of it, some are not. Either way, we probably don't want to believe it, but the truth is that we would not treat ourselves this way unless somewhere deep inside, we hated ourselves. The hatred may be obscure, may be hidden, but it is operating inside us as that inner destructive energy, the source of the violence that powers these painful behaviors.

RECOGNIZING HATRED

If we are not yet certain that hatred is the fuel, the driving force, we can ask ourselves, "How could I reject myself if I didn't have that kind of heartless disregard for who I am? How could I reject my experience—try to push it away, resist it, twist it, and manipulate it—if somewhere in me I didn't have an unfeeling, heartless energy that is not attuned, not sensitive, to the effects of that rejection?"

To absorb this recognition in a way that will help you to understand it better, take a moment to consider what we have discovered so far in the chapters that have led up to this point. Much of the work we have been doing is to support our understanding of the nature and the effects of various types of negative reactions to our experience. Manipulation, control, resistance, defensiveness, judgment, comparison, rejection—all of these are our attempts to get rid of experiences that we don't want. From this perspective, we will be able to see that hatred is the ultimate expression of all our negative reactions, and in fact, is the root of these behaviors.

So how do we identify that hatred in ourselves? Often it will not be obvious, but you will find that it is easiest to recognize when you feel the quality of obsessiveness. That's because when hatred is present, obsession is also present—our consciousness is consumed with the object of our hatred. Let's say that somebody has emotionally wounded you. You will probably find yourself obsessing, thinking, "What am I going to do? How am I going to get that person?" All kinds of images go through your mind, and you can't stop trying to figure out the most damaging thing you could do to that person or to imagine the worst thing that could happen to them. Or maybe you keep obsessing about fairness, justice, and retribution in the situation. If you look underneath all those thoughts and schemes, what you will find is hatred.

We tend to want to use other terms for what we are feeling because we are more comfortable with them. We might say, "I feel a lot of aggression toward that person," "I can't stand him," or even "I'm really angry with her." Or you might put a more positive spin on it and say, "Well, it's my responsibility to protect others from getting wounded in the same way I was." Those things may be true, but when you are obsessive, the issue really is one of hatred.

And if we see this as the hatred that powers the inner activity fundamental to ego, then it is evident that it is actually hatred of life—the uncontrollable, dynamic flow of life. In the realm of inner work, this hatred is directed toward our own experience, toward ourselves. So, we need to recognize and understand our hatred, see its manifestations, and see how it acts to try to change our experience. When you say that you want to reject your experience, change it, or make it better, the inner impulse is actually to obliterate it, to destroy it, to make it not be there, because it is not wanted.

Before we try to understand what this hatred actually is, it's important to be aware of how we are influenced by the way hatred is generally viewed in our society. Almost everyone has been taught that hatred is bad, wrong, or evil—something to be avoided because it harms others and ourselves. But as we have seen, being with ourselves as we are requires a more open and accepting attitude toward all of our experience. This is not a matter of endorsing any particular way of being, feeling, or acting. It is a matter of encouraging exploration. So, accepting our self-hatred in the truest sense doesn't mean that we are saying that it is good or right; it just means that we can be with it and explore it without judgment, trusting that whatever we need to see and understand about it will be revealed through the wisdom of our True Nature.

DISCERNING WHAT
HATRED IS

So what *is* hatred? If we try to see what is behind it, we will notice that hatred is an attempt to remove difficulties. Hatred is an attempt to get back at what hurts us, what obstructs us, what prevents us from getting what we want. It is an effort to remove the impediment, the frustration, and the source of that frustration. So hatred is inherently vengeful, but it is also an attempt to redress the situation. You want to balance things out, and you think that will happen only if you can remove the source that hurt you.

Obviously this experience of hatred and vengefulness operates between individuals and between societies, but here our focus is on how it operates inside us. Hatred is an energy we unleash on any experience that we consider to be a source of frustration.

So when we don't like or accept what is arising within us— whether it is anger or sadness or weakness or deficiency, or even a positive feeling such as love or kindness—we want to destroy it because we feel that it is objectionable. But the deeper issue is this: Because such an experience or feeling is objectionable, we conclude that it is preventing us from being happy, from having what we want. We tell ourselves, "This experience is not what I want, so I am not happy because of it; it is my enemy. I am therefore going to obliterate it." And how do you obliterate it? You hate it. Hatred is the most effective thing that ego has come up with to obliterate the enemy.

History has demonstrated what we have also discovered internally to be true: Hatred is a particular energy that can destroy because it doesn't have heart, it doesn't have love, it doesn't have the sensitivity and the attunement of kindness and gentleness. It is a very effective instrument of destruction. But it is effective at the expense of our sensitivity, at the expense of our attunement, at the expense of our awareness and consciousness. It obliterates by removing sensitivity. So it tends to diminish and limit our awareness, to flatten it.

THE MYTH OF EGO
ANNIHILATION

We can see this loss of awareness in the way hatred arises in the context of our inner work. As we go deeper in our inner practice, we begin to recognize that what stands in the way of our spiritual realization are our ego manifestations—our issues, our contractions, our resistances, our conflicts, our identifications—in short, our ego-self. We have learned enough to recognize that it is the self that is keeping us from simply being. Now our hatred manifests as an attempt to destroy that self—and we think that doing so is serving a spiritual truth!

Because so many spiritual teachers have said that the way to realization is to annihilate the ego, and that ego death is the answer to all our problems, we may not have examined yet the implications of this teaching. What does ego death mean? It usually means to us, "Eliminate the ego; annihilate it. Destroy the self, because for us, as spiritual seekers, it is the enemy."

What do we do with an enemy that is in the way? We do whatever we can to take the enemy out, to get it out of the way so we can reach the nirvana that we want. We are looking for the final release, because we believe that once the impediment is gone—once the contractions are gone, the frustrations are gone, the issues are gone, the ignorance is gone, the ego is gone, the self is gone—then we will be happy, we will be enlightened, we will be at peace.

Here we are seeing a specific expression of the same tendency that is there all the time—the desire to obliterate whatever we don't like in our experience or about ourselves. When that tendency is extreme, people consciously hate themselves to the point of depression or even suicide. But inherent in all ego activity—whether we're dealing with daily challenges, a serious psychological crisis, or our spiritual practice—is a subtle hatred driving the inner activity that is always attempting to bring about happiness and "the final release."

Think about it. Why do we want to change ourselves? To feel good, to feel better, to finally be at rest. Consider all the movies that focus on eliminating the bad guys or getting revenge. What happens when the hero finally kills the bad guy or puts him in jail? Peace and relaxation. But it is only at the end of the movie, in the last couple of minutes, that the hero can stop all his incessant activity and finally rest. The whole movie is about getting to the point where he can just let go and relax—put his feet up and drink a beer. Before that, he is obsessed with the enemy: "I have to get rid of him. I have to finish what I set out to do; otherwise, I can't have any peace." This is the perfect expression of our inner conviction about how we arrive at peace and rest.

We see this engrained throughout human society. For example, when I listen to the news and hear about so many murders, rapes, and abuses, I notice that it's often the family of the victim who is most emphatic that the person who committed the crime get the maximum punishment, even when that is the death penalty. The family members openly say, "We want satisfaction," and the law supports that—society itself supports their position.

The idea that if we are wronged, we are completely justified in our desire to hurt the other, to get back at and punish that person has been institutionalized in our society. Even nice, ordinary people say, "I can't rest until I get satisfaction. That man murdered my child, so I have to put him behind bars or in the electric chair. Only then will I be satisfied." I always wonder why that is satisfying. Where is the satisfaction in killing somebody else or hurting them as much as possible?

We think that it will be satisfying because that is what our hatred wants. It is our hatred in action. The only way we believe we can live at peace with ourselves is by eliminating whatever it is that hurt us, whatever caused us misfortune, because we want to get back to that peace of mind, to that nirvana. We want to get rid of it, forget about it, relax, and go on with our lives.

So, hatred is pandemic, it is everywhere. We hate others when we feel wronged or frustrated. And what we feel toward others, we inevitably feel toward ourselves. Why is that? If we hate someone else, we are hating the fact that they have hurt, humiliated, or frustrated us. We want to annihilate them so that we will no longer experience these feelings. This means that we actually hate our own feelings that we believe are caused by that person. So hating an object reflects the fact that we hate the feelings that object engenders in us, and hence we hate ourselves.

At a deeper place, hatred implies self-hatred because hatred itself already reflects a duality: There is me and the other or me and what I hate, which is bound to be a duality within the self as well. Since in truth we are not a duality—we are an expression of the beingness of everything—if we hate anything, we are dividing ourselves, our awareness; we are hating part of our own consciousness. And we are separating ourselves from the oneness of our nature. It cannot be any other way.

DISCOVERING HATRED

As we become more aware of the issues related to hatred of others and hatred of self, we pass through many stages and recognitions. It is only at the deeper stages of inner practice that we come to recognize that we hate ourselves explicitly. See if you can identify where you are and what is true for you in relation to the following statements. Some are sequential, and some overlap.

- I am disregarding or shutting someone out for slighting me, but do not believe that I actually hate him.
- My thoughts about not acknowledging this person are becoming obsessive, and I recognize that I actually do hate him.
- I recognize my hatred for this person, but do not recognize that in hating him, I am also hating myself.
- I cannot see my self-hatred in explicit ways, but I can notice my tendency to reject myself, judge myself, attack myself, criticize myself, and try to modify, change, and improve myself.
- I notice that my inner activity has become obsessive; that I can't stop rejecting, judging, criticizing, and trying to change and improve myself.

- I am aware of the particular struggles I face, and I still believe that I am justified in my efforts to change myself; that it is the primary means to achieving my peace of mind.
- I begin to recognize that a primary result of my inner activity is that a certain feverish inner state is maintained, and that dynamic feels unstoppable.
- I see the incessant activity of my ego as the central impediment to my peace. It is my enemy; I wish I could get rid of it. I believe that my spiritual practice can help me eliminate my ego so I can be free.
- I get so frustrated with my constant agitation, with the fact that I am always doing something to myself. I can't do anything to stop that, so I can never settle down and have peace.
- I hate the unstoppable activity that goes on inside me and I want to destroy it. *I hate myself.*
- I didn't realize this before, but now that my hatred has shown itself, I see that it has been there all the time.

THE CAUSES OF HATRED

We can say that our problem is the ego, the self, but there is no ego or self except what manifests in our consciousness. To understand how hatred functions, it helps to know how it got there. Generally speaking, the causes of hatred originate on two levels. The first level, which I call the psychodynamic, relates to our personal history. From the time of our childhood, we have not been sufficiently loved. Maybe we have been hated, disregarded, humiliated, or treated as though we didn't exist; maybe we've felt guilty or bad, or hated ourselves for things that were done to us or that we have done. The frustration that develops in us through interacting with our environment plus many of the things we learn from others generate a lot of hatred. The specifics vary depending on the circumstances of one's life, but it almost never happens that someone escapes the effects of hatred.

The second level is our lack of understanding, our ignorance about how consciousness works. We can recognize that there are obstacles to our freedom, barriers to our inner peace that make it seem impossible to just be ourselves without struggling all the time. But, as we have seen, because we don't understand how things function, we end up believing that the way to deal with these impediments is to get rid of them—to remove or annihilate the obstacles, just as we tend to do in the physical world. This is the only way we think we can have peace and quiet and release from suffering. We don't know that by doing this, we are perpetuating the same suffering, the same frustration. We are dividing ourselves and acting inside ourselves in a destructive way. Our actions dissociate us from ourselves and prevent our True Nature from revealing itself in its purity and richness. So we get stuck in a misinformed, misguided attempt at realization, at freedom, at achieving nirvana.

We are ignorant of how reality works. And it takes a lot for us to learn it. But with time and practice, wisdom begins to arise just from our observing what is happening and from learning about our True Nature. We start to see that the inner activity we are engaging in to remove obstacles actually imitates a power in our True Nature that can eliminate obstacles. This power is needed because obstacles such as ignorance, identifications, barriers, and resistances definitely exist. But we need to learn that the way of the ego doesn't work, because ultimately it is based on hatred, and hatred is divisive.

These divisive strategies of the ego make us callous—they actually move us further from Being. But once we see that they are attempts to do something that the ego is not capable of, then we have the chance to recognize what *Being* can do. We are able to realize the power True Nature has that can reveal clearly what is occurring, that gives us the precise understanding of the impediment—what it does and why it is there. And if we recognize the impediment for what it is—with the complete immediacy of presence and the precise clarity of awareness—that awareness itself will appear as a quality that is pure stillness, that is pure peacefulness, that is the presence of peace.

The presence of peace alone dissolves all agitation. Peace doesn't have to do anything; its mere manifestation melts all strife, and impediments simply dissolve through the understanding that is inseparable from that stillness.

That is why this teaching keeps emphasizing just being there, not doing anything, and simply being vulnerable to and present with immediacy of feeling. If we are being there with immediacy of feeling and not doing anything, at some point that not doing reveals its power. This power is not just that we refrain from taking action, but that we experience the presence of total stillness. This is the essence of nondoing, which *is* peace. Just the fact of stillness, the presence of peace, annihilates ignorance. But *this* annihilation is the action of appreciation and love in pure nondoing and stillness.

Hatred wants to annihilate, but it annihilates by destroying, by making our awareness dull, by suppressing, by dividing. True Nature does not really annihilate, because something is not wiping out something else—there is no duality. The kind of annihilation that True Nature makes possible is more of a recognition, a precise understanding that Being reveals in us. We have no inner agitation in our attitude; we see and understand whatever impediment is arising, but we do not give it energy in the form of reaction, and thus it becomes still on its own and does not reappear. We experience this as a dissolving or a melting, but what is actually happening is that the energy fueling the obstacle disappears, the obstacle loses its dynamism, and it simply stops arising.

What happens at this point is that we recognize that the stillness or quieting of the ego, of the self, is not separate from the stillness of our Being. And we discover that we are in the state that the ego wanted to achieve but could never reach because its method of pushing things away and trying to destroy them doesn't work. What works is just simply being with a clear awareness of what is happening.

We are ignorant of our Being and its power, but it still exists somewhere inside us, so on some level we do know what it is. Because we are ignorant of this power, we set about creating another power—hatred—which is a distortion and an imitation of the true power. The aim of hatred is to remove our suffering, to remove the impediment. And we believe that it will eliminate the obstacles between us and the riches of our Being. But as we have seen, when we try to do that by fighting, by rejecting, by trying to blow up the enemy, our efforts end up perpetuating the violence, the agitation, and the separation from Being.

So how do you cease this destructive inner activity? First, you need to recognize your resistance and your rejection, and the hatred that is implicit in these attitudes. Because the hatred is the energy that drives the rejection, the rejection won't stop as long as that energy is there; so you need to become aware of the hatred. Thus you need to relate to your hatred and self-hatred in the same way you relate to rejection, resistance, or defensiveness when they arise: You don't reject the hatred; you recognize it for what it is. Rather than acting it out or having it dominate you, you become the awareness that holds it.

Learn to hold your hatred, be with it, feel it as much as possible from the inside and from the outside. Seek to know hatred, to feel the energy of it, to feel the power of it, and recognize all the associations that come up in relation to it. See into the history that created it and understand that, too. Continue in your inquiry until you are finally able to feel that hatred completely, in its full energy and power. If you do not obstruct it through judgment or rejection, the hatred will—just like anything else that arises in your experience—naturally reveal its own nature. It will dissolve, leaving what is true.

And that truth turns out to be essential power—it is the power of truth and peace and stillness. This is the immense and silent power to *be*—to be undisturbed and unruffled by the ignorance and reactivity of the familiar self. It is simply the power to be who you are, without domination or control, the power of True Nature that brings a love and a freedom in simply being yourself.

EXPLORATION SESSION

Identifying Self-Hatred

The purpose of this exercise is to open up your curiosity and willingness to see the hatred that may be operating unconsciously in your inner practice. To do this, you want to explore the ways you attempt to change, modify, improve, or enlighten yourself. Consider the whole range of internal activities you engage in, such as comparing yourself to standards, analyzing your behavior, managing your emotional reactions, stopping your inner process, and limiting your awareness.

Reflect on the underlying best intentions that you may have, as well as your convictions about what it takes for you to change or grow. Notice the degree to which you are either willing to be open to yourself as you actually are or trying to make yourself fit your ideals of how you should be. Pay attention to any inner sense of ruthlessness or viciousness or coldness in the process of inquiring. Also note any discomfort, fear, or shame that may arise as you explore.

The more you are willing to see the manipulations, judgments, attacks, and rejections—whatever manifestations of aggression are part of your inner process—the more you can recognize the energy that is the driving force that powers them. Be aware that hatred may manifest as rejection, disregard, violence, obsessiveness, agitation, withdrawal, coldness, or lack of feeling, as well as the direct annihilating intensity of pure hatred.

When you can recognize an element of your own self-hatred, notice how it makes you feel to be aware of it. Can you understand it enough not to judge yourself for its presence? If there is some space to be with the hatred, see what happens if you simply stay with the experience while being present with yourself.

CHAPTER 10

Ignorance and
Direct Knowing

IN THE FIRST PART OF THIS BOOK, we explored how the obstacles to self-realization arise in our practice of just being where we are. We focused on the ways in which aggression, attachment, defensiveness, resistance, rejection, self-hatred, and other types of inner activity make it difficult for us to be whatever we are, wherever we find ourselves.

What may not be clear yet is that none of these activities can be understood fully until we recognize their relation to ignorance. For example, when hatred arises, there are psychodynamic or historical learned reasons for it, but they are not the only causes. Hatred also arises simply because we are ignorant. That is, we don't know how our mind functions, how our consciousness functions.

This brings us to the necessity of examining the primary root of the ego, of all ego life, which is ignorance. Just as we need to be aware of the specific manifestations that make it difficult for us to be real, to be ourselves, we need to see the contribution of our ignorance to this situation. When we discover how ignorance underlies all these inner activities and related attitudes, we realize that it is the fundamental impediment to being where we are.

Without ignorance, it would be difficult to continue these activities. That's because as ignorance dissolves, insight and self-knowledge arise. We need to be clear about how our ignorance operates so that as it transforms, we can understand how it becomes insight, clarity, knowledge, and the recognition of the truth of a situation. Enlightenment means waking up to reality, recognizing it as it really is and being there with it as it is. That is why enlightenment is usually understood as self-knowledge, self-realization, illumination, clarity.

In prior chapters, we have worked with the fact that we have all kinds of beliefs, ideas, positions, identifications, and structures that we take ourselves to be. And we have seen that these are not who and what we are. We've also worked on our unconsciousness and its issues and how what arises in our experience is associated with these unconscious parts of ourselves, making it difficult to know the truth of our experience. So, although you may not have realized it, much of the inquiry we have already done has actually been inquiry into ignorance as it manifests in these different ways. Let's look more deeply, then, into the situation of ignorance.

LEARNED IGNORANCE

There are two kinds of ignorance that we need to recognize and understand so that we are no longer controlled and defined by them. Once we see them for what they are, they stop being obstacles.

The first kind is called *learned ignorance*. It can also be referred to as *developed ignorance* or *accumulated ignorance*. Sometimes the term *conceptual ignorance* is used, which means that as our mind develops and we acquire the capacity to conceptualize, we develop a certain kind of ignorance that is specifically human. Generally speaking, animals and other beings don't have that type of ignorance, because it is something that you have to learn in order for it to develop.

Usually this ignorance develops as knowledge. That is to say, much of our knowledge about ourselves and about the world is actually learned ignorance. It is ignorant because it is simply wrong; it does not reflect how reality is. We have all kinds of beliefs and ideas about reality that are not true. We have positions and philosophies and ideologies about ourselves, about how things work, and about what makes things happen, and many of these are inaccurate. Of course, it is difficult to see this as ignorance, because it is what we know, it is what we take to be our knowledge.

Even our experimentally verified scientific knowledge is part of this learned ignorance. Although it is useful and in some sense correct, it is not a true picture of how things are. But generally speaking, our problems are not related to the accuracy of scientific knowledge; they concern our personal knowledge about who we are and what we are, what reality is, what relationships are, how things happen, how the mind works, and so on.

For example, a lot of people believe that hatred, power, and aggression will bring us peace and freedom—but it doesn't work that way. That kind of ignorance is very difficult to dispel. But the fact is, any kind of ignorance is difficult to dispel. When you believe something is true, many people can tell you that it's incorrect, but you don't believe them. You keep behaving as if it were true, because you really believe it *is* true.

So our learned ignorance underlies much of our inner activity and our external actions. A common example is comparative judgment. We think we know what is good, what is bad. We imagine that *this* is what should happen or *that* is what should have happened. These suppositions are based on the ignorance that we call knowledge. Not only do we believe we know what should happen, we also think, "I know how to bring it about. I just need to visualize some kind of angel or deity" or "I need to get involved politically, meditate more, breathe more consciously, deepen my inquiry, feed the hungry, go back to school . . ." It goes on and on.

So, to summarize the characteristics of learned ignorance, we can say that:

- It is our accumulated knowledge about reality. It is what we take to be true, and so it forms the basis for our inner and outer activity.
- It is also called conceptual ignorance. We conceptualize things in our mind, and these things become knowledge, and that knowledge becomes the learned ignorance.
- Even though much of it is scientifically accurate, it is not how reality is. This doesn't mean it contradicts reality, but rather it is an approximation of it.
- When it comes to our knowledge about ourselves and our consciousness, how the soul and awareness work, what we take to be real is simply not true. Often, it's the opposite of the truth.

As you have seen, much of the inner work consists of seeing through all our identifications, our structures, our beliefs, our positions, and our self-images that we have taken to be real. For example, we believe that we are this individual with this history who is interacting with other individuals with their histories. We believe we're physical bodies that move through time and space, and we take that to be knowledge because it can be scientifically verified. But through the work of inner realization, we recognize at some point that this is a learned knowledge, which is really a learned ignorance, an accumulated ignorance.

We come to recognize that what we take to be true is false, is not the whole truth, or holds a meaning different from what we think it is.

INNATE IGNORANCE

The other level of ignorance is more fundamental, more subtle, and more difficult to deal with. It is called innate ignorance. But we cannot even recognize it as ignorance until we work through much of our learned ignorance. Unless we become much more illuminated about our beliefs, ideas, positions, and patterns, our innate ignorance will be hard to identify. But at some point, it becomes clear that no matter how much of our learned ignorance we work through, the realization arising from that process does not bring us to the clarity, openness, and immediacy that we have experienced when we are more directly in touch with reality. This is when we begin to recognize what is called *innate ignorance,* which is also referred to as *primordial ignorance.* This is the ignorance that we share with all animals. It is not learned; we come into the world with it.

Learned ignorance is directly connected with development of the mind and the ego—with all the structures and representations, images, patterns, beliefs, and ideas about oneself and reality. But the development of that learned ignorance is based on a more fundamental ignorance—the ignorance of our True Nature.

We come into the world not knowing our True Nature. We don't know who we are. That doesn't mean that we don't experience True Nature. It doesn't mean we don't feel it. It doesn't mean that we don't perceive it. It means we don't understand it. We don't know what it is. We don't know its meaning, its significance. We don't know that *it is what we are.*

Animals are their True Nature, but they don't know it. Very young babies are almost purely their True Nature, but they don't know it either. When we are infants, we might feel it, sense it, taste it, but we don't know that it is what we are. To know the significance of it, to be able to discriminate it in an insightful way—to recognize, "That is me! That is the nature of the world. And that is the truth"— we first need to develop learned ignorance.

So to clarify the relationship between learned ignorance, innate ignorance, and our True Nature, we can say:

- Learned ignorance is based on innate ignorance; without that innate ignorance, we cannot develop learned ignorance.
- We have to develop learned ignorance before we can recognize our innate or fundamental ignorance.
- The reason we form an idea of who we are—which becomes part of our learned ignorance—is because we don't know our True Nature; we are innately ignorant.
- If we knew from the beginning who and what we are, we would not need to develop a sense of self in order to know who we are.

But we don't know who we are, so we do develop a sense of self and we believe it and we take it to be true because of our innate ignorance.

• As we work through the learned ignorance, we begin to experience our True Nature. To understand our True Nature fully, we have to go through our innate ignorance. To go through our innate ignorance requires that we fully understand True Nature.

To begin to challenge innate ignorance means learning to recognize something that we don't even have a category for. It's just like seeing something exotic for the first time. You see it, you experience it, but if it is subtle or is there all the time, you don't recognize what it is. You don't realize the significance of what you are seeing. For example, people from temperate climates who visit far northern areas see snow as simply snow. The natives, however, live with snow most of the time and are familiar with many variations of coldness, dryness, texture, and density and thus see many different forms of snow, hardly considering them all to be one thing called snow. Only over time, and with the demands of experience, would the newcomer be able to recognize snow in all those variations.

As an adult, you won't know what True Nature is without guidance or a true curiosity to learn. If you're too young, you won't know what it is because you don't yet have the capacity to recognize it. The capacity to discriminate and understand requires a certain level of mind development. However, as the mind develops, it develops with learned ignorance.

DEVELOPING OUR CAPACITY
FOR DISCRIMINATION

The ego develops with the mind, and as that happens, our discriminating capacity grows. Babies already have some discrimination, but it is far more rudimentary than our adult capacity to tell things apart, to know what they are, and to recognize their significance and their relationship to other things. Babies' discrimination is just the possibility of recognition. All of it is hard-wired recognition and instinctual cues. But we know now that babies do have a kind of knowingness that is operant much earlier than developmental psychologists used to think.

It takes time for the mind to develop the capacity for discriminating knowledge, and though researchers may not agree on the exact timing, it is agreed that this development happens in stages. We all start life with inherent ignorance—we know that we are, that we exist, but we don't know *what* we are. We experience, but we don't know what we experience. We see, but we don't know what we are seeing. In time, we learn what things are, and we also learn how to recognize, how to discriminate, how to tell things apart and know them. All of this develops the capacity of conceptualization.

How does this happen? We develop our capacity by coming to know the usual things that people know. Phenomena at the most obvious, gross level—the physical level—are paramount at the beginning. So we begin by knowing our bodies, knowing other people, knowing things in the physical environment, and so on. And this is followed by increasingly more subtle kinds of knowing.

As we have seen, by the time we have developed our learned, conceptual knowledge, it is really learned or conceptual ignorance, because it obscures the True Nature we started with. Our learned ignorance veils and disconnects us from who we really are. To recognize True Nature and have it available to experience, we need to penetrate and see through our learned ignorance. But to *understand* True Nature, we need to overcome our innate ignorance.

UNDERSTANDING
OUR TRUE NATURE

How do we come to understand our True Nature? And what does it even mean to understand it?

There are three aspects to understanding our True Nature. First, we need to know what True Nature is. Second, we have to recognize it as our own nature, not as something outside of ourselves or as an abstraction. And third, we need to understand the relationship of our True Nature to the rest of manifestation—to the thoughts, the feelings, the body, the objects we see, and so on. To know what True Nature is, to know that it is what we are, and to know its relationship to everything in manifestation—that is full understanding. That is illumination. That is enlightenment.

Each of these three steps brings us toward more complete understanding. And each step of understanding is more difficult than the one before it. So, we might recognize True Nature, but be unaware that that is what we are. Or we might recognize True Nature and know ourselves as that, but we might not yet know how it relates to everything else. Let's look at these three steps in more detail.

The first step is to recognize what True Nature is. This means to distinguish it from more familiar elements in our experience such as thoughts and feelings, sensations and energy. We need to see how it impacts our perception and affects our relationship to our experience. We must know that True Nature is the fundamental nature of experience and understand what that means in order to recognize it *as* True Nature.

The second step is to understand *yourself* as True Nature. This means having full discrimination and insight, at the adult level, into who and what you are. It is possible to recognize True Nature—the first step—but not know that it is you. You might think it's God. Or that it's an angel who has descended into the room. You experience that this presence is empty and light and luminous, and it feels so different from how you know "yourself" that you think it must be some kind of wonderful angel. You recognize that presence, but you don't know that it's you. To understand yourself as True Nature means that you recognize, "That is *my* nature." And this occurs not through thinking, but through experiencing.

The third step is to see that True Nature is the nature of everything and to know how it manifests everything. We don't know how things work because we don't understand how things are related to True Nature.

Seeing the relationship of True Nature to everything else will help us recognize and understand how things work. How do things happen? What is action? How does action occur? How are action and inaction related? Understanding these things is essential to the wisdom of living. If you're just sitting and meditating, you don't need to know True Nature's relation to everything else. But we don't just sit, we live. Our mind functions with all its thoughts and feelings. We need to understand the relationships that exist within all parts of our life.

MOVING THROUGH IGNORANCE TO TRUE NATURE

We have talked about ignorance and how it functions as an impediment to enlightenment, to knowing our True Nature, to living in the freedom of True Nature. Our practice of inquiry is fundamentally to help us see through the ignorance, to recognize it *as* ignorance. As ignorance is recognized as ignorance, it will transform to true knowledge, to the perception of the truth.

What is the process by which this occurs? We always begin our inquiry by seeing what is true in our experience. I might recognize, for example, that what is true is that I don't like the way a friend is ignoring me. By exploring that truth, I might come to see that I don't like it because it is similar to the way my mother ignored me, which made me feel worthless. So I believe, in relation to this friend, that I am a hurt child and she is my mother. So, we can see in some detail what accounts for our feeling one way or another. The truth we see at first is the truth about what is not true. We recognize the false as false. As I see my self-image and the projection on my friend, it becomes clear that neither is really true. She is not my mother, and I am not that image of a worthless child. I am actually something more alive and immediate, a presence that has inherent value because it is what is real.

This brings us then to recognizing the truth—recognizing what we are actually experiencing and recognizing that truth is our True Nature. We discover that that is what we *are*, not just what we experience. Many steps and experiences of being with the truth as it reveals the false or learned ignorance may be needed before True Nature is revealed as our nature. And love of the truth must be our guide. Ultimately, by staying with the process, we arrive at the third level of understanding, where we see and know that True Nature, our True Nature, is what moves everything—that it is the source of everything.

How does this discovery happen? By simply being where we are. Throughout the journey, whether we're inquiring or we're meditating or just going about our business, we're learning to be present and aware, to just be there, not doing anything to anything. This attitude invites True Nature to reveal itself, to reveal that it is what we are, and to reveal how everything else relates to it.

IMMEDIATE KNOWINGNESS

So, as we see, in some sense, our practice is a matter of self-knowledge, self-illumination. It's enlightenment, a knowing. The knowing we're talking about here is not conceptual knowing, remember. Conceptual knowing always becomes conceptual ignorance. Even if you know something that is true, even if you recognize something about your True Nature, the moment it becomes conceptual and gets filed away in your mind, it becomes an image. If you take the image to be reality, or start to see reality through that image, it becomes a veil again. It becomes ignorance.

So, the knowingness we're talking about has to be immediate. That's why we say you not only have to be aware, you have to be fully present. Your consciousness of what you are experiencing has to fill the entire field of your awareness. It has to feel whatever is there, without veils or filters. Whatever you are feeling—hatred, rejection, resistance, anger, happiness, spaciousness—you allow it to fill all of your awareness, so that you feel it directly and completely. And the feeling of that, the experience of whatever is arising, is inseparable from the knowingness of it—because you cannot know True Nature conceptually, through the discursive mind.

Nevertheless, the development of the discursive mind is a necessary stage in developing the discriminating capacity of our inherent awareness. And it is useful for performing the tasks of life. But it is not the kind of knowing that is needed for realization. That kind of knowing has to be more of a felt knowing, an experiential knowing. I call it immediate or direct knowledge.

In the West, we have a word for it—"gnosis," which means "knowing." But gnosis is a knowing through Being, through immediate contact in which the feeling and the experience of the knowing are inseparable. So, we need to refine our language and understand the terms in a way that makes our discernment more attuned and more acute. By seeing the nature of gnosis—the direct knowing that confronts our ignorance—we can appreciate that it is nondual knowing. We move beyond the duality that pervades our perception and our usual knowing of the mind. This in turn makes it more possible to see and recognize True Nature.

That is why our practice of inquiry is an inquiry into our experience. That is why our meditation is the immediacy of Being, which is the beingness, the presence, and the awareness that pervades the presence. And the awareness that pervades that presence creates the possibility of recognition, of direct knowing, or gnosis. When that capacity for recognition is developed, and we are experiencing True Nature, we can recognize that that's what we really are and that it is actually the nature of everything.

What you don't see, doesn't develop. If you don't recognize a particular part of your experience for what it is, it will not reveal itself completely. So the potential in human beings to know their True Nature cannot be realized in an infant or an animal because neither one can recognize True Nature for what it is. We need to recognize it for it to unfold. The more we recognize and understand True Nature, the more it reveals its possibilities.

So, being seen, being known, being recognized and discerned, invites True Nature to further reveal what it is. It reveals its treasures, its fullness, its perfection. That knowingness liberates, because it helps us to see what we are, what we're doing, and how things work. That's what is meant by becoming wise. We are more consistently able to recognize when we are rejecting or interfering with our experience and are more able to stop doing that. We become more and more capable of letting ourselves be who we are and what we are—our True Nature. So in our practice we are learning to be wise. We're learning wisdom through directly understanding our experience.

EXPLORATION SESSION

Recognizing Learned Ignorance and Direct Knowing

Find a quiet place to consider the world around you. First open yourself to an immediate awareness of reality both outside and inside, with a focus on sensation and perception. Just notice colors, shapes, textures, sensations, and patterns in your experience. Be aware of your usual way of recognizing all the objects in your experience, but refrain from getting involved with the content and stay attuned to your perceptual awareness.

Then consider how your ideas, beliefs, and knowledge about that reality impact your direct experience of it. When you focus on the content of what you are aware of, what happens? Do mental concepts enhance your experience? Do they fill in detail? Do they shape or focus your attention in a particular direction? Do they distance you from the immediacy?

When you stay with the direct perceptual experience, what happens to your knowing and understanding of your experience? Does it disappear without the ideas? Does it manifest in a different way than the knowing in your mind? Consider the difference in quality between your familiar mental knowing (the learned ignorance) and this more direct experiential knowing.

CHAPTER 11

Freedom from the
Filters of the Mind

OUR DISCUSSION OF IGNORANCE as the fundamental barrier
to being where we are has moved us into new territory that we
will now begin to explore more fully. Rather than focusing on the specific ways that we react to our experience, we will be examining the
obstacles that are inherent in the *way* that we experience. These obstacles are not the specific activities of rejection, interference, manipulation, and other secondary manifestations we have observed that
comprise our reactions to the main event. Rather, they are misunder-
standings or misperceptions of what it is we are actually experiencing—of where we are and who we are and of reality itself. In turning
our attention to these obstacles, we shift our focus from the secondary
manifestations of our experience to the primary manifestation—how
the experience itself is actually arising and being perceived.

Let us review what we have explored so far, so we can see more
clearly the transition into this new territory:

We have continually pointed to "not doing anything" and "being where we are." These are two different ways of saying the same thing. Each one clarifies something about ourselves. "Not doing anything" means not engaging in inner activity of any kind. "Being where we are" points to the fact that the *absence* of this inner self-centered activity is what we mean by presence, or Being. So, we have seen that if we really learn not to do anything to our own experience, we are simply there. Conversely, if we are really being where we are, we won't be doing anything to our experience.

We have discussed some of the ways that we meddle with our experience—how we don't leave it alone, how we try to change it, make it better, improve upon it, judge it, reject it, push it away, pull on it, and so on. It is useful to note here that becoming more aware of how these activities act as barriers or blocks doesn't mean we are doing something. We are simply developing more discrimination to help us with our practice. We are only learning what it means to really stay where we are—how to be present in the moment and be ourselves.

We have discussed how our learned ignorance, which is what we believe we know, forms the basis for all of our interference. We have seen how our activities and relationships are based on ideas and beliefs and identifications—what we think is true, what we think is reality, what we think will work.

But all of these activities that we have examined are of a certain type. They tend to be more explicit and more easily identifiable—although, as we have seen, they often can be subtle. And they are also secondary manifestations—various reactions to what we perceive our experience to be. But there is another category of interference with our experience that is much more difficult to see. It is interference within and inseparable from the primary manifestation, that is, in the way we perceive what is immediately occurring. It is the second major way that our accumulated knowledge becomes an obstacle to being ourselves—through a much more subtle way that we interfere with our experience by trying, consciously or unconsciously, to direct it, and thus prevent it from emerging spontaneously on its own.

What I am referring to is an implicit, inner activity that we may become aware of as we become increasingly skilled at not going along with the more explicit, grosser inner activities that we have identified. It is the way that our mind or consciousness influences and molds our experience, just because it is involved in that experience. Let's take a look now at how this operates.

VEILS OF THE PAST

We can see the movement of projection or judgment. We can hear, feel, sense our hate and our rejection. But this other category of activity cannot be as easily identified. At first, as we engage in it, we will think that we are just being where we are and are not doing anything. But as we notice and observe our reactions in different situations, it becomes possible to begin to see that much of "being where we are" is still the result of interference.

Why is this kind of interference so difficult to perceive? Partly because the more explicit activities of interference occur intermittently, and thus are easier to notice when they arise. This other kind of interference is a more subliminal, sometimes even unconscious, inner activity that occurs all the time. Its usual explicit manifestation is our continuous thinking process, our almost constant inner dialogue. We can sometimes notice it as an agitated, energetic quality inside us, though we may not be clear what is creating it. But whether or not it comes to our attention, it affects our experience, molding it one way or another according to our accumulated knowledge—which is based on our ignorance. Hence our experience is not free to spontaneously manifest exactly what it is, or more accurately, what it can be.

Here's an example. Let's say that you are having an interaction with another person. It doesn't have to be a highly charged situation; any interaction will reveal that you are reenacting a familiar pattern. You see the person in a certain way, you see yourself in a certain way, and you feel a certain way about how the two of you are relating. But even though your experience seems to be simply what is happening—you believe that you are just being where you are with that person—it is really formed by your accumulated knowledge and memories.

The way you experience the interaction—and, in fact, almost any interaction—is a reenactment of an internalized experience of someone from your past. You are projecting the dynamics of an earlier relationship onto the present one and perceiving the present interaction through that veil. What is happening is not freely, spontaneously arising; you are forming it, you are making it be a certain way. And one indication of this is the fact that somebody else wouldn't experience that person in the same way.

You won't see yourself as trying to be a certain way. You will think, "I'm just being who I am," but it is not truly a spontaneously and freely arising experience. It is determined by your historical knowledge, your learned knowledge—all the beliefs and ideas about who you are and what other people are like and what reality is. It is influenced by your ordinary accumulated knowledge.

So, looking at this situation of interference with all its subtle activity, we can see that:

- Our experience doesn't freely arise. We interfere with the spontaneity of our experience by perceiving it through our accumulated beliefs and understandings.
- Specifically, our experiences are molded and formed by a subliminal mental process—the incessant activity of remembering, thinking, and reacting according to information from the past.
- In any interaction with another individual, we impose on our experience an image of who we are, an image of the other person, and a particular feeling tone on the relationship itself. The result is an experience of reality created, at least in part, by past conditioning.

- We don't see our activity as an interference because we are not explicitly rejecting a particular experience. But what we are actually rejecting is the spontaneity of our arising experiences. This is exactly the difficulty we have in being where we are: we try to direct our experience. But here we are not just *trying* to direct our experience, we are *actually* directing it. We are shaping it by looking at it through the past. Our experience is partly formed by it emerging through the filter of past knowledge.

- This is a subtler inner activity to observe because it is an almost continuous, subliminal, or unconscious mental process with many parts: remembering, imagining, imposing a particular image or form, filtering, projecting, and a host of other subliminal mental and emotional operations.

We can see from this that we are continually creating our experience instead of letting it be itself, instead of letting it emerge freely on its own. Thus all ego experience is inherently an interference with our present experience. Here is another example:

Let's say you are feeling, "I am furious at my partner; that is where I really am." It seems to be the truth, and it probably is. But being furious at this person may also imply that you have imposed on the situation a relationship from someone else in your past. You dragged that out of your memory, carried it on your shoulders, and have attached it to the moment. You forced it on the moment, and you keep forcing it on, keep trying to make it stay, so that it conforms to the past that you are still carrying.

So you have your story: "I'm furious because this person did this hurtful thing to me." Most of the time, however, when we explore the situation, we find that we are not seeing the matter correctly. And even if some of what we perceive is true, inevitably we are also projecting onto the experience things that aren't really happening; we are in at least partial delusion.

This is another way of saying that we are doing something to our experience. But it is a kind of doing that we don't usually see as doing. We say, "I can't help thinking that I am really furious at this guy," but the thinking itself is an interference with the moment. It is a reacting and a remembering. We are activating a particular program that we think of as reality.

It *is* our reality, on one level, but if we let ourselves really be there with that reality, if we are present and feeling that reality fully, it can take us further into the truth, and the experience will begin to reveal its True Nature. We will start to see that our thoughts about a person we are angry at involves a mental operation, a projection, a transference, and an imaging of ourselves. In other words, in order for that experience of our being furious to happen, we must believe that we are a certain person and our partner is a certain person. If we let go of those beliefs, the reality will begin to shift. We may not believe we can let go of those beliefs, which might be true. But the important awareness is that our reality is at least partly based on a mental belief carried over from the past. So we become able to see the mental quality of our experience, which exposes its empty quality—its lack of presence—because the reality we are experiencing lacks full immediacy.

That is why awareness with presence is emphasized as our practice—being aware of and present with where we are. If we are only aware, but not truly present, we might miss the fact that our experience can be palpable, full of consciousness—that we can have an immediate contact and in-touchness with whatever is happening.

Let's review, then, how we move toward a transparent understanding of our experience and toward being who and what we really are.

- As we experience an event or interaction, we are generally reacting to what we experience happening (secondary manifestation). This involves judgment, resistance, denial, manipulation, and so forth.
- When we can stop this interference, we become more aware of what is actually arising (the primary manifestation) and begin to understand it. We see that it is not a full, immediate experience

of the now. We recognize that we have layers and layers of veils over our experience that make it not completely palpable, not completely alive, not immediate.

- We think we are being where we are, but we are actually engaged in an inner activity that is at first not obvious. We are unconsciously disconnected, dissociated from our Being, or we might have some sense of disconnection but feel that we have no volition in the matter.

- If we just stay present with our experience and do not fight it, it begins to reveal itself, and we start to see how our mind is meddling with our experience in the moment.

- As we see how our beliefs and ideas are involved, we begin to see the mental quality of our experience, its emptiness and its lack of reality.

- We superimpose on the moment what we believe we are. In other words, whenever something happens, we react in a certain way based on a certain projection from the past that makes us be a certain kind of person at the moment.

- As greater clarity, greater understanding, and greater awareness of presence arise, we begin to recognize that when we think we are being where we are, we are not being ourselves yet. We begin to see that what we are engaged in is a reaction, a projection of our mind onto the moment.

- We begin to see more specifically the inner activities of primary-manifestation meddling, which we have been accustomed to believing are the real content of the moment. We become aware of our self-images, our identities, our ego structures, the programming from our personal history, and our projections. All of these are interferences.

- As we come to understand what is happening—by recognizing that the content of the experience is a projection and a position we are taking in the moment—the light of awareness transforms our experience into the actual reality of that moment. At the same time, it will transform us into what we really are, not what we believe ourselves to be.

EXPOSING THE LACK
OF IMMEDIACY

As we work through these issues, it becomes clear that our ignorance perpetuates itself because we don't know who we are. So how do we understand and work with this kind of inner activity that keeps us from really being ourselves?

This activity is very difficult to perceive because, as we said, it is subliminal and mostly unconscious. One traditional method we use is to sit in meditation, which means to not engage intentionally with any inner activity. Eventually, the mind will quiet down, the agitation will settle, and that settling, that quietness, will begin to bring more immediacy to our experience. Actually, it will first begin to reveal the lack of immediacy, and then it will bring about more immediacy. That is because in meditation, we are not dissociating from our present moment through the mental processes of thinking, reacting, and inner agitation.

In terms of the primary practice of being where you are and inquiring into your experience, you will find that it is best to work with the immediacy of your experience, bringing to it a quality of awareness and consciousness that can look into the truth of it. You engage with your experience, inquire into it: What is it? What is its nature? What is making it be the particular way it is in each moment?

We see our thoughts, our feelings, and the content of our images and projections and through contrast and scientific comparative judgment, we can perceive the connections between these elements and what we have experienced in the past. You might see, for example, "Oh, how I'm feeling right now is similar to how I reacted to my mother when she used to tell me that I'm stupid."

In making this kind of connection, we recognize something common to all our experiences—that they are not truly of the moment; they are colored by our past. We can see the veil, the wrapping that our consciousness has put around itself, which has become an interference. We recognize that the dynamism of our Being is not completely free; the total openness that invites experience to arise freshly, just as it is, is missing. We sense that our experience is occurring through old, musty filters that create a dullness and a darkness.

We often talk about being here in our ordinary experience. And of course, we *are* being here in some sense. But what does it mean to be here in the first stage of self-discovery, when there is no direct sense of essential presence? All it means is that I am feeling what I am feeling and I am not overtly trying to change it. But *I* am not being there yet! How can I be there if it is just an idea of me who is there? All I can do is to be aware of what is happening, to feel it, to recognize it and not fight it.

However, if I truly learn not to fight it, my experience begins to reveal that I am *not* being here, I am not really present. It is true that I am not fighting it, I am aware of it, I am not trying to get away. So I might not be off somewhere else with my attention, but I am not really here either. I haven't really landed in the truth of what is here, the truth of the now. I'm just hovering over the experience. I am someplace in my mind, in a mental reality.

REIFYING OUR EXPERIENCE

We see that when we examine the mental content of our experience, we begin to notice that our experience is composed of images, reactions, and projections that are all knowledge in our mind. A simpler but more profound way to say this is that our experience is composed mostly of reifications. A reification refers to something that we have experienced or thought about that has become an object in our mind, a mental construct.

For instance, the body image that we rely on to experience ourselves is a reification of the body. When you see somebody that you know walking by, you see them as a particular physical time/space entity, identified by a certain label called a name. This is a reification—an encapsulated idea of what a person is. But a person is not a time/space entity. He or she is a manifestation, a form that reality assumes that we first experience at a specific point in time. Our mind remembers that impression, abstracts it out of the oneness of Being from which it is inseparable, and makes it into an object, putting a wrapping around it and labeling it.

Let's say that you are having a meal and you lift your spoon. What is this spoon? The spoon that you are experiencing is not the real spoon. What you are experiencing is the reification of the spoon— that is, something that your mind is imposing on the situation. You are mentally creating an object that we call a spoon and projecting it onto the form that reality is taking in the now. If you could see this form without the reification, without that mental operation, you would recognize it as presence assuming that particular shape and color at that location.

I don't mean that there is nothing real about the spoon. Obviously something is in your hand that you are using to get the food to your mouth. But if you see the spoon without any mental operation, it will be more like the appearance of a spoon, a hologram of a spoon. Actually, without reifications you will see that it is light. It is a form of light with shadows and colors, stripped of its familiar mental-image identity as a spoon. And it is the mental imaging of the spoon that makes it opaque and solid to the eye. Without those reifications or mental images, everything around you would become one vast field of light shaping itself into holograms. But usually, because of our reifications, we don't see the light itself; we only see the color and shape the light takes, which we then label as this or that object. This mental object is an opacity that cuts us off from contact with the field of light.

Extending the example of the spoon to the rest of our experience, we can see how our learned knowledge becomes an obstacle to being ourselves. Our entire experience is composed of reifications—abstracted concepts and impressions that have become mentally created objects. We keep imposing our belief in those entities on our experience. This is how we interfere with the moment, making it appear as though these entities were real, when it is really our mind that has made them into entities.

This process of reifying our experience is ongoing and constant, and we are continually imposing old reifications from the past. We do not see the now; rather we experience a reified moment, which means that we are superimposing previously created reifications—images, representations, and mental constructs of what we think is the self, other people, and various objects, on the now.

Because we are tightly wrapping the moment with these constructs, the dynamism of Being is not free to manifest itself in us. Our Being, then, is always constrained and directed to manifest through one kind of wrapping or another that is specifically ours. This reifying of experience, of awareness, of the present moment, prevents us from being ourselves. We don't feel that we are really there. It's as though we haven't landed. We feel that way because there is a dissociation—a distance between our true beingness and what we are experiencing—that is created by the mind interposing layer after layer of these wrappings.

We have learned in earlier chapters that our practice is to see the truth about what is happening in our experience in each moment, to recognize what it is and understand it. Now that you have some understanding of how reification operates, you can appreciate how important it is to feel our way through that process, to approach it experientially. Because if we only work with it mentally, we are still operating within our reifications and will remain trapped by them. That is why it is not possible for the thinking mind alone to dissolve reification, despite the claims of some postmodern philosophers.

In contrast, observing our experience with awareness and with presence challenges the reifications by revealing them *as* reifications. It is our belief in them that keeps them in place. We hold on to them, we preserve them by believing that they are real. But once we recognize them as mental constructs, they become transparent, and that makes it possible for us to stop going along with them.

It is important to remember here that whatever constructs we identify are not to be treated as the enemy and rejected. Just as in any other part of our practice, we are called to understand our mental operations and recognize our lack of immediacy and the reifications that create it. This occurs simply by being present and aware of what is happening and inquiring into it. Even when we recognize how we are limiting our immediacy, we don't have to fall into the trap of judgment.

As we recognize these things for what they are, the obstacles, the layers, begin to dissolve, and we begin to experience ourselves as more landed, more present. As they dissolve, they reveal the True Nature of the moment, and we feel a greater immediacy in our experience.

Eventually, we recognize that immediacy really means presence. That is, when our experience becomes truly immediate—without the interposition of any mental construct—then we are here, really in the now, fully in our experience. To be in our experience in this way is what we call presence and that is what we mean when we talk about truly being ourselves. We realize that "being here" means, "I am actually the presence that I am. I am here at this very moment, and my experience is not a mental construction dredged up from my past. I am just what I am in my factness, and I am experiencing this moment completely, directly, without anything intervening. I am the very awareness, the very consciousness, that is present, that exists, in this very moment, and I am experiencing myself as that very existence."

Further, when we are no longer defined and restricted by the constructs that our mind has imposed on the moment—when we finally can experience ourselves with immediacy and let ourselves be—we recognize what it means not to act internally, on ourselves or our experience. Because "not taking any inner action" and "being ourselves" turn out to be exactly the same thing—the simplicity of just being here.

And then the realization arises: "Not only am I free to just be, free to not act; I am the aware medium, the conscious medium itself." That fact, and the recognition of that fact, is what makes it possible for us to be truly where we are—which turns out to be *what* we are.

We also come to understand what immediacy is. That is, we experience things directly. But we also recognize that we are experiencing ourselves in that immediacy. We do not just experience the content of the experience; we are experiencing our awareness as well.

So if I am experiencing my sadness in some moment, and I am able to do that with immediacy, totally, I then recognize that I am this presence, this fullness, this awareness, this luminosity, that is pervaded at some location within it by the affect of sadness. I am that self-existing awareness that is aware of that sadness.

And we recognize that this self-existing awareness is now the primary arising in our experience. It is an actual true manifestation of reality in this moment. Everything else—including all of our feelings—is secondary and is always changing.

Further, when our experience is truly immediate in the sense that the experiencer and the experienced are in total contact, with no distance between them, then they become one, and we experience that oneness as what we are: "I am just here, I am just what I am." But what that means is that the I that exists—that is here, that is what I am—is not an idea, not a construct in the mind; it is the very awareness, the very presence, the very palpable consciousness that is made out of luminosity, out of the clarity of Being.

This is a deeper understanding than we have reached before about what it means to be where we are. We can see more clearly now the connection between being where we are and being ourselves, being real. We can recognize that "where I am" means that I—my true self, my awareness, my presence, my very existence, what at this very moment *is* in this moment—am aware of and am the awareness of all the details that are arising within the content of my experience. And I am aware of all of that with immediacy, with an awareness that pervades it completely.

So, early in our practice, immediacy might appear to be just our inner experience, but eventually all experience becomes immediate. Every time we experience something, we experience the very substance of that something because we *are* that very substance. We can more clearly understand now how "being where we are" is only separated from "what we are" by the activity of the mind. Truly, we are what we experience.

EXPLORATION SESSION

*Observing What Enhances or Limits
the Immediacy of Your Experience*

You can do this exercise by looking at the way you respond to other people you are relating to, by examining your inner experience when you are not interacting with another person, or some of both. Take some time to reflect on the following questions:

What makes your experience more immediate?

What are the ways that you limit the immediacy of your experience?

What causes you to limit the immediacy of your experience?

What's right about limiting the immediacy of your experience? That is, what benefit do you believe you gain by doing that? In exploring this question, you are addressing your unconscious, not your logical mind.

How are you limiting the immediacy of your experience right at this moment?

CHAPTER 12

The Trap of
Identification

IN THE PRECEDING CHAPTER, we saw that all our ordinary
knowledge is based on the subtle mental operation that we call
reification: taking an experience, a perception, an impression, or a
concept and objectifying it, storing it, and then using it in various
situations as a lens or filter for our experience. We learned that our
ordinary experience is mediated by this activity of the mind that
is constantly filtering our perception and forming our experience
according to our accumulated knowledge and history. In this chapter,
we are going to take another step toward understanding more specifically how this process works.

For our reified knowledge—our learned ignorance—to form our
primary experience or our secondary reaction to it, a specific mental
process needs to be in operation. Continuing from our perspective
of learning to be who we are, where we are, let's explore what that
process is.

IDENTIFICATION
IS THE OBSTACLE

The fact that we have reifications in our mind does not in itself create an obstacle to being where we are. Our reactions, our associations, or even our rejection of a feeling or experience, are not in themselves obstacles to being ourselves. We have to use our reifications in a particular way for them to become impediments. An example from everyday life will reveal why this is so.

Let's say you are at a party with your husband or wife and you notice out of the corner of your eye that across the room, someone is flirting with your spouse. Your spouse is warming up to that person, obviously enjoying the attention, laughing and behaving in ways that don't happen with you. You find yourself having the reaction we call jealousy.

Usually, people are totally taken over by the experience of jealousy, but it is actually possible for jealousy to arise without it influencing you in a way that hooks you. If you pay attention, you will see that jealousy can arise as an image, as a thought, as a feeling, or as certain physiological responses in the body. So you could recognize jealousy to be simply the arising of a particular state that you are experiencing. It is possible to be aware of whatever manifestations of jealousy are arising and choose to experience them fully, allowing your awareness to make them transparent. If you could be present in the awareness pervading it, jealousy would transform itself, naturally and spontaneously, to reveal its underlying nature.

However, we usually end up using these experiences in a way that traps us; we get stuck not because of the feeling itself but because of how we are relating to it. We are not just experiencing jealousy; we are burying ourselves in it. We define ourselves by it: "I am a jealous person and I know that is who I am." Sometimes we recognize that jealousy is controlling us and determining our feelings and actions, and other times we are taken over so much by it we don't even know that we are jealous. We just express it in our behavior, words, and actions.

We call this *identification*. It's not just that jealousy is happening; it is that we are *identifying* with the state of jealousy. The feeling is actually just a momentary wave, but we don't see that. We don't see that we are something bigger that contains this feeling, that the feeling itself is a much smaller thing than we are and doesn't define us. If we were not identified, we could understand our jealous feeling as something that floats in and floats out of our consciousness. But when we are inside the wave and defined by it, we forget about the ocean; we even forget about the water. Thus, it is this process of identification that is necessary for any piece of old knowledge—any reification—to become an obstacle.

Of course, many mental processes are involved in identification, including remembering, integrating, comparing, projecting, representing, reifying, and so on, but usually these are all referred to by one simple heading—identification.

ALL EGO EXPERIENCE IS IDENTIFICATION

It is not only difficult or distressing feelings that tend to draw us into identifying. All ego experience includes identification; we are always identifying with one kind of content or another. So the first thing to notice is that we can identify ourselves with just about anything. It could be an ego structure or a self-image, a projection or a particular emotion, habitual feelings or thoughts, a desire or an attachment, a plan or an idea or an ideal. It can be a large thing, a small thing, a mental operation, or something concrete. The identification can be a gross, obvious entrapment or it can be very subtle and in the background. Our identification can be based on the past, and it can also be an identification with present experience itself.

Because identification is so pervasive, we want to better understand this subtle activity in which we are constantly engaged. We want to know more about this habit that traps us in a limited, momentary manifestation, while in fact our fundamental nature —our true identity—is actually something completely free, something vast. So we begin by looking at the definition of the term *identification*.

IDENTIFICATION AS PRESENT-TIME ACTIVITY

The word "identification" as it is used in psychological literature is taken to mean the use of an image, impression, or representation to define our sense of who we are or our sense of reality. In other words, we take an image, impression, or piece of knowledge, and we make it into a basic building block of our sense of self. This is part of the process of the development of the ego—internalizing impressions, stabilizing them inside the mind, and using them to define who we are and what the world is.

The way we use the term "identification" in our work includes this psychodynamic meaning, which views identification mainly as a historical process. But it also includes present-time activity: the action of identifying in this very moment. For example, we might be identifying with a particular structure that was formed by our ego in the past and has remained unconscious, such as "I am a strong woman" or "I am a stupid kid," and we identify with it, which means that we believe that it is true—"that is what I am." We are living out of that identification, moment to moment, even if we are not saying those words to ourselves.

IDENTIFICATION WITH THE BODY

With this definition in mind, we can see that a more pervasive though subtle example of identification has to do with our own body. It is clear to us that we usually identify with our body; we take our body to be what we are—it is our identity, our very self. We are not only experiencing the body, we are not only aware of the body, we are using the body to define us. In fact, it is hard to consider identifying who we are without including at least subconsciously our experience as a body.

We act as if we were the body, and so our identification with it is ongoing, almost totally continuous. The body is happening this very moment; it is not just a memory, and it is not static. But we identify with it as if it were fixed. So what we are really identifying with is a body image—the image of our body that we have constructed in our mind. This is something from the past that is remembered and brought to bear in each moment. We actually feel our body according to that image. But even if we felt our body in its immediacy right now, we could also identify with that and limit our sense of who we are to only that experience.

To understand identification more clearly, let's contrast how we feel about our body with how we feel about our clothes. We may be attached to some of our clothes, but we usually don't identify with them. That is because we change them many times, and they get old and worn, or we just get bored with them, so we give or throw them away and get new ones. They don't define us. But my body is not something I'm going to exchange for a new version—even though certain people do think of getting a cloned body, and increasing numbers of people are paying large sums of money for surgery to change the appearance of various parts of the body. The very fact that people are willing to do and spend so much to change their body is indication of the degree to which they identify with it.

So it is with our body, not with our clothes, that we tend to have the strongest, deepest identification. That is not to say that we don't ever identify with our clothing. We may have an attachment to a certain dress or suit, but identification with our clothes is usually in relation to a style of dress rather than to particular items of clothing. In that sense, your style does define you. For example, a woman may be attached to wearing baggy old clothes. If her friends suggest, "Why don't you wear something more fashionable and that fits you better?" she won't do it because it doesn't fit her self-identity; she is identified with her casual, loosely fitted style. Other people always have to wear the latest fashion—that's part of their identity—while others love to dress with a studied eccentricity that makes them feel unique.

Let's say the eccentric dresser is attached to a particular item of clothing. If she were to lose it, or it got ruined at the dry cleaners, she would be upset. She wouldn't give a favorite piece of clothing away, and she probably wouldn't want to lend it out. This is more of an attachment than an identification.

Although attachment and identification are usually not the same thing, they can overlap. This is because identification is both a way we define who we are and a way we invest ourselves emotionally and energetically in something. The latter sense of identification is quite close to the meaning of attachment. Thus, we can see that some attachments are the same thing as identification. For example, we are attached to our body but we are also identified with it. We definitely don't want to give it up—partly because we have invested so much of our life in it, but also because we believe it is actually who we are.

IDENTIFICATION WITH
THE EMOTIONS

We can experience the same kind of strong identification with an emotion. As we said earlier, the difference between identifying or not identifying depends on our response to the content that is arising, not on the content itself. So when I am feeling angry, I can be identified with the anger, which means, "I want to be angry. I have to be angry. I am going to continue to feel angry. I can justify why I am angry. I have all the right to be angry." If I am not identified with the anger, I can say, "Okay, so I'm angry; that's just what is happening right now. What's the big deal? I get angry a lot; it comes and goes." So, now we can see the basic principles of identification:

- To identify means that we define ourselves with something—who we believe we are is not separate from that particular impression or manifestation.

- To identify can also mean that we are emotionally and energetically invested in that impression.
- It is our relationship to what arises that defines whether or not identification happens and what form it takes.

IDENTIFYING WITH
THE PRESENT MOMENT

Identification most often happens in relation to events, structures, images, and beliefs from the past, but we can also identify with present-moment manifestations that are not reifications. Suppose you experience your True Nature and feel the presence of it as clarity and lightness. Simply *being* that spacious, clear presence is not the same as *identifying* with it. That's because being your True Nature does not involve a mental operation; there is just the recognition that "this is what I am in the moment." Now, you could identify with that presence once you recognized it, but identification adds something onto it. The mind comes in and holds on to the experience and becomes stuck in it. The mind wants to grasp it, to use it to identify who you are.

So even when we are being ourselves, experiencing the presence of our True Nature, identification is still possible. To identify with that pure presence implies a reifying process, that is, turning the experience into an "object" that can be identified with in some way. Our mind recognizes True Nature, but it doesn't stop there. It wants to put True Nature in some kind of package. Then it attaches itself to that experience in a particular way that enables us to form an idea of who we are.

From this, we can see that:

- Identification always implies reification.
- If we don't reify our experience, the mind can't identify with it.
- Identification can occur whether the reifying process is the result of something from the past or of a new experience happening in the present moment.

- Identification happens because we believe that we need to have a self and an identity for the self.

You can see now that when you are identifying with something, you are being taken over by the content of the experience or the feeling. But even knowing that is not sufficient to understand completely how identification functions. You need to be able to distinguish between being taken over by an identification that binds you and being taken over in a way that allows you freedom.

Consider that when you are being True Nature, you are also taken over—but you are taken over and free. You as you usually conceive yourself to be no longer exists. There is just True Nature. In identification, on the other hand, an ego identity—a sense of self—is attaching itself to or defining itself with some kind of an experience or the content of that experience. And the identification is always with a reified content.

This is not to say, however, that you are not supposed to feel things. If you are sad, for example, instead of rejecting your experience, you could welcome the feeling, experience the immediate fullness of sadness, without identifying with it. And the only thing that can do that, that can completely pervade sadness, is presence itself. When we see a limitation of our ability to do that, we recognize that the presence is limited in that situation.

IDENTIFICATION SUPPORTS
FALSE IDENTITY

If I am being my True Nature, it is not an identification; it is just simply being, which is not an activity. Now the word "being" is a little tricky in English. Because the verb is "to be," "I am being" implies that I am *doing* being. But that is not what the phrase means. It means that I am not doing anything to be myself. I am just myself. I don't need anything to be it. I *am* it. However, when I am it, there is nobody, no I, that is being it. There is no separation. I and it are one thing; there is no I to claim it. So, when I say I am the light, I am the presence, I don't mean that there is an I that is identifying with light or presence. It is just a recognition, a knowingness, a seeing, an awareness of that which is here.

However, the mind can suddenly come in and reify the content of such an experience by recognizing it as an object of perception, putting a boundary around it, and using it at that very moment to create a sense of self. Thus, I become attached to the experience and I identify with it.

In contrast to being, identification is an activity, a mental action that I engage in to connect myself with something. If I identify with what I am, I first have to believe that I am separate from what I am in order to enact identification.

So, this is one of the central dangers on the spiritual path: whenever we experience something new, we want to put it in a box. We reify it and then separate from it in order to identify with it. Students sometimes ask me, "I had such and such an experience. What is it? What do we call it?" They ask in part because they want to recognize what has just happened to them, but they also ask so they can label and define their experience and hold on to it. The idea is: "If I can package this really nice thing that happened to me, I can identify with it—I can think that it is me, that it is part of me; it's something I can say I have." True presence, on the other hand, doesn't care what it is. It is totally uninvested in itself. It is simply being itself.

We can become aware of the tendency to want to freeze-frame our experience so that it can be known. Having all these snapshots is how we reify, but reality is more like a movie than a still picture. When you are being, everything is flowing.

IF IT'S YOU, YOU CAN'T LOSE IT

When we get identified, we don't feel as though we have done it ourselves; we feel that something has happened *to* us. But in fact, identification is something we do. And it is possible to become aware of this subtle inner activity and what is behind it. When a strong identification occurs, it is almost like an addiction; you feel a need to be identified.

But it is not just a need for this or that particular identification. What you believe you need is an identity. You are addicted to having an identity, and it is very difficult to be totally without the identifications that are continually creating that identity. And we are identified with so many things at the same time. One identification drops away and another one takes its place. We shed one after the other, but our need for self-identity remains.

Identification can happen with anything. Some people are identified with their jobs. Most people are identified with being a man or with being a woman. We believe that if we drop the identification, the reality will drop off. But, in fact, whatever is truly real is not created or maintained by our identification with it.

When we are being ourselves, implicit in that is the trust, the security, the certainty, the easy, natural, relaxed way of simply being there. The recognition of this is the illumination of who we are. Thus, if I know completely that this is who I am, I don't need to engage in a mental operation to establish it or try to remember it. And if I really recognize that it is me, I don't need to remind myself that it is me. Wherever I go, it is me. But if I am not confident that it is me, then I will struggle to remember who I am.

Another way to say this is: if we don't have that certainty, if we don't trust who we are, then we reify ourselves so that we carry an identity around with us. And we go around asserting it to others. Some people are identified with being the Absolute, and if somebody tells them they are not the Absolute, they feel wounded. "Can't you see that I am? Everybody should see that I am the Absolute!" That can happen to spiritually advanced adults. But this means that there is an identification. And even though the person might be actually experiencing themselves as the Absolute, the identification creates a gap, what I call the narcissistic gap. In that gap of needing to be seen as what we are, we are not being completely ourselves, we are not being where we are. We are not simply being.

Every kind of identification is a mental operation that traps us into a particular form. Some of us identify with our nationality. Some of us are identified with our race. Other people are identified with their intelligence or with their beauty. We know that many of us are identified with being a child or with being an abused child. What is important to remember is that every form keeps us trapped, no matter how lofty it may seem. We are not free regardless of what we identify with. I can experience myself as God, but if I am identified with being God, I am lost, I am not free. Then I have to be God and everybody had better know it.

DISIDENTIFICATION AS PART OF SPIRITUAL PRACTICE

No matter what form identification takes, it always arises out of the particular relationship we have with the content of our experience. We make that specific content important in a way that disconnects us from the immediacy of being ourselves. That is why many spiritual traditions train their students to learn to recognize the identification and undo it. Or, more accurately, they teach them to recognize the identification and not go along with it.

Many people think that disidentification is an activity: "I see my identification, and I do something to it—I disidentify. In the same way that I identify, I can disidentify." But this is not the case. Identification is an activity, and true disidentification is the absence of that activity.

Disidentification means:

- Recognizing the inner gluing of my identity or consciousness to a specific content
- Seeing this adherence to the content for what it is—an identification
- Not believing the identification or going along with it
- Not pushing it away

- Understanding it and letting it dissolve or reveal itself as True Nature

If we try to push an identification away, we end up identifying with something else. True Nature doesn't push anything away. When it sees identification, True Nature says, "Hmm, that's a very interesting manifestation. I didn't know I could do that! I can actually trap myself. And sometimes I even forget that I trap myself. I am good at trapping myself."

So it is important not to associate disidentifying with the inner activity of pushing away or disowning. Some people, for example, are concerned that if they don't identify with their values, their values will disappear. Not identifying with your values doesn't mean that they will go away. If they are real, they will be there; in fact they will be there more strongly. If they are not real, they will go away. But that only means that you are not completely certain about the reality of your values. And that's why you need to identify with them. Identification says, "I am not willing to give the thing up! I am not willing to be free of that identification." This is exactly why identification has such a grip on us: we don't want to give up our identifications because it would feel like a loss of ground.

IDENTIFICATION IS NOT YOUR NEMESIS

Like anything else that arises in our experience, we do not need to make identification our enemy. Identification is not your nemesis; it is not something you have to fight. It is something to be aware of, to recognize. Because if you fight, if you make it your nemesis, then you are engaging in the same activity—you are just identifying with something else. If you're angry, you can get trapped in thinking, "I am not that; I am my True Nature. I shouldn't get angry in the first place. And I definitely shouldn't be identified with my anger now that I am feeling it."

Or we reject other people. Let's say you and your best friend are talking and you end up in an argument. You say to him, "I think you're identified with your anger." When you say that, you are most likely *not* saying, "I'm aware of your identification and offering you this information to help you liberate yourself." What you are really telling him is, "You'd better not keep this up; I don't like it. I want you to get away from me because I want to liberate *myself* from your anger."

IDENTIFICATION AND INQUIRY

What are the implications for our practice of inquiry? Now that we understand that any reification, any structure, that we are trapped in implies an identification, we can learn how to more easily recognize when we are getting caught in identifying. The more we are present, and the more we are aware of the present, the more we can settle down and allow the natural unfoldment of our experience. As our awareness becomes stronger, it will become easier to have a direct, immediate knowingness of our experience. Certainly our mind will label our experience; that is its natural tendency, and we don't need to fight that either. But it can be more of an afterthought, and it does not have to interfere with the inquiry. What we inquire into is our immediate experience that the mind labels. That immediate experience is what unfolds, and that is where the inquiry stays.

If, on the other hand, the focus is more on the discursive mind that is labeling, then actual inquiry is not occurring; it is more of a mental inquiry that will not help us learn to be where we are. We will stay dissociated instead of learning to be real.

What we have been discerning in this chapter is one of the most pervasive and subtle forms of how we manipulate our experience and distance ourselves from the immediacy of where we are. Identification is an inevitable result of our mental capacity to objectify our experience combined with our lack of trust in simply being. Our ability to attend to this activity, to be curious about it, to learn how it works and to not go along with it, will directly increase our capacity to be the simplicity of our True Nature.

EXPLORATION SESSION

Recognizing Identification
in Your Experience

Take about fifteen minutes to make an open inquiry into whatever is happening to you, moment to moment. At any given time, you are likely to be identified with some element of what is going on. As you inquire into your experience to see where you are, consider how identification may be shaping that experience.

In order to recognize your identification, you need to see where you are coming from or who you take yourself to be in the midst of your experience. Being aware of reactions, attitudes, desires, preferences, and attachments provides clues that can help you recognize the way you are identified.

If you become aware of an identification, notice how you feel when you recognize it. Do you judge it, reject it, feel relieved, get curious? If you are able to explore it, notice if it shifts, dissolves, or transforms over time. Being aware of the variations in your sense of constraint and freedom as you inquire can be another clue to the activity of identification.

CHAPTER 13

Lighting Up the Now

I F WE EXPERIENCE OURSELVES in our true self-existing condition, we will see what we actually are: We are beings of light. Remember the example in chapter 11 of the spoon, which, when seen without any mental operation of reification, is perceived to be a form of light. We, too, are forms or beings of light when we experience ourselves with total immediacy.

We are beings of light in the fluid state—completely frictionless, completely luminous, totally radiant and free. Now, everybody knows that because light has no mass and no weight, gravity does not affect it. So, in our True Nature, we have no heaviness, no thickness, no weight. We are substantial only in the sense that fluid light has a fullness, a sense of body to it. But that fullness, that substantiality, is completely light and smooth. That is the nature of awareness. And because it is light, it doesn't *help* us see—*it is what sees*, it is what perceives. Thus light, awareness, consciousness, perception, sensitivity are all the same thing.

However, even if we recognize the truth that we are beings of light, we tend to reify that perception and identify with it,

153

concretizing ourselves and experiencing ourselves as heavy and opaque. Even as beings of light, we see ourselves as a physical body, with its parts and activities, having mass and operating under the influence of gravity. We think that we are entities in space and time, and that our existence began in the past and will end in the future.

In our continuing exploration of True Nature and of the obstacles to being ourselves that we encounter, we want to focus now on another particular area that makes it difficult to be who we are: our incomplete understanding of the nature of time. In order to do this, we need to observe our experience from the perspective of being a being of light. What are the properties of light and time that can help us understand more about our essential nature?

LIGHT AND THE PASSAGE OF TIME

Science tells us that light moves at the maximum speed possible in the universe, which endows light with certain properties that differentiate it from everything else. One of the principles within Einstein's theory of relativity is that the faster one travels, the slower time passes. Time slows down for somebody who is going at a very high speed—and the closer we get to the speed of light, the slower time becomes. That means that the closer we come to being light, the slower that time will pass for us.

What are the implications of this for understanding what it means to be ourselves? If we apply it to our internal life, we can see that the more we are present and the more fully we are experiencing and being our essential presence, the more we will experience things slowing down. This seems to be a law of time—not that linear time is being altered, but more time becomes experientially "available" to us. Thus, the slowing down of our experience of time will place us more and more in the present. The more we are the presence, the more we are in the present. So, the slowness of time has a lot to do with being in the present.

There is most likely an etymological connection between the words "present" and "presence," because the two are very much connected in sense and meaning. In our practice of inquiry, when we talk about being where we are, we mean being in the moment. Our experience is always in the present, even though our mind might be flitting about in the past and future. The actual manifestation—what is arising in our experience—is always arising right now. This is also true of light. For light there is only now; there is nothing else. This fact is another consequence of the reality described by Einstein's relativity equations.

What is behind the principle that the faster you go, the more slowly you experience time? It begins with understanding that the speed of any object in the universe can be seen as a function of traveling in both space and time. We never travel in space without time passing. Physics has determined that the faster you go in space, the slower you go in time. As we travel at normal speeds, that is not apparent to us. But as objects accelerate and approach the speed of light, it becomes apparent that speed in time slows down the more speed in space increases—the maximum point being the speed of light.

In our universe, nothing can exceed the speed of light in space. And the slower you travel relative to the speed of light, the faster time passes. So for human beings, time passes very quickly relative to light because we move very slowly in space in comparison to light. Thus the combination of speed in space and in time always equals the speed of light.

LIGHT AND THE ETERNAL NOW

The human experience is of moving about in space and steadily, constantly aging—of having time pass. What is the experience of light? Time does not pass for light—light does not go through time. It travels at the maximum speed in space—the speed of light. So what is its speed in time? Zero. That is, since its speed in space is the speed of light, and the speed of light is the maximum speed, its speed in time is zero.

Einstein was talking about physical light, but when we are experiencing the inner light, the actual luminosity of our True Nature, we begin to appreciate Einstein's idea and have an actual experience that is analogous to it, instead of just a theoretical understanding of the idea. We begin to know what it means when we say that for light, time does not pass; that for light it is always the eternal now, and there is nothing but now.

What does that mean? If you see light from a star, and some of it is coming from as far back in time as the Big Bang, you will think that the part of light that you are seeing is very old—say, three billion light years old. Logically, you think, "This light came from that star and it took it that long to get here, so it must be at least that old." The light itself, however, will not experience that any time has passed for it. If you were to experience the light, or if you were "riding" the light, you would know that it is the same age as it was at the time of the Big Bang. It is one hundred percent new light, ever fresh; it never gets old.

So for humans, who are operating outside of light, time passes, and things get old. For the light, there is no such thing. Light travels through space at a certain speed, but it has no experience of getting old. It is always new, always fresh, and so it is always itself; it doesn't change. It is always, always, its very nature.

You might not have thought about that, but scientifically, it is known that light is ageless. We don't experience that because we are not traveling with light; we are looking at it from outside. This is just like looking at our True Nature from the outside, from the perspective of the physical body: We keep experiencing the passage of time, and therefore we assume that time must pass for our True Nature, too. But if we are in the stance of our True Nature, things can change around us, and our body still changes, but the experience is that there is no passage of time. And that is because the experience of that body of light is agelessness, endlessness—always now, now, now, never changing, that ever-fresh now, this very moment always.

So what we call present time is actually the intersection between what we call time and that timeless presence. The only place we touch True Nature is in the present moment, not in the past or the future. In the present moment is where True Nature intersects time, because it is the now.

NOW WITHOUT FUTURE

True Nature is the now-ness of time, but the now-ness of time is not just the present time, the particular moment you are in. When you experience the actual now-ness, it is not an instant *in* time; it does not have a beginning or an end. If you notice an event happening, you can say that it has a beginning and it has an end, but all of it is actually experienced in the now. So the now itself doesn't start with the beginning of the event and it doesn't end with the end of the event. It is always now.

You can see, then, why it is difficult to think logically from the perspective of light. The universe appears differently for light. As we have seen, light doesn't age, and time doesn't pass for it. So there is no such thing as boredom, because there is no history, and there is no such thing as future.

What does that mean for us as human beings having experiences? If there is no history, no future, then nothing affects me. How can I be affected if it is only the now that is real, that is present? And if I recognize that there is only the now, what is the point of trying to change my experience?

Any attempt to alter your experience, to improve it means that you believe that there is a future and you are living for that future. You are saying no to the now out of hope for some better future. But for light, that better future never comes. Whenever we want to advance to a better future, we disconnect, we cut off from the path of light. Light experiences only the now, the very moment. It recognizes that what is now is what is, that what reality is is the now-ness of this moment.

Even if you just look at this logically, what else is there but now? The rest of it is really just stories in our mind. If you believe the stories of your mind, you believe in past and future as possibilities.

LIVING IN THE NOW

So this is where we can see how our orientation, our attitude, about time can become an obstacle, an obscuration, to being our True Nature. If we have the attitude of future orientation, we miss the moment. We are dissociated from the presence of the moment, and we can't be in the moment.

The truth is that our True Nature is similar to the nature of light, which is timeless and which we can experience *in* the moment as the now-ness *of* the moment. But if we are oriented toward the future, we are not allowing ourselves to be where we are, which is now, and we are also leaving, dissociating from, the moment. Our nature is light, pure now-ness, so to operate from the perspective of a future that can get better or worse means that we are dissociating ourselves from our True Nature. How am I going to be myself if I do that? How am I going to be where I am?

In other words, the orientation of hope—hoping for something in the future—disconnects you from who you really are. The orientation of expectation or of having a goal to accomplish does the same thing. For example, you may be thinking that one of these days, you are going to be enlightened, so you are working at it now. Light would never think that way; it doesn't posit an end state in which everything is going to be wonderful, and it doesn't say that we have to practice now in order to get to that goal. For light, that is completely nonsensical; there is just now. Now is just wonderful the way it is, and now is all that we have.

If there is future in our life, it is true that we need to consider it for the sake of practical matters. When you are doing your budgeting or choosing insurance policies or making travel arrangements, you will have to include the future in your planning. But what does that have to do with your experience of yourself in the moment? Your experience in the moment is your own consciousness, which is a fluid body of light. Why can't you experience that even as you are planning?

The way we relate to facing the experience of death is an important example of what I am talking about. If you are totally in the moment when death comes, it won't be a terrible thing. It is true that it will be a shock to the system, but the fear that most people in our culture have about death is about more than that. It is our fear of being totally in the moment, any moment—without past or future—that makes us afraid to face the particular moment that we call death. Death is a moment with no future. Likewise, it is the fear of physical death that makes us afraid to be completely present in each moment. Why is that? Because totally letting go of the past and the future is a death of the familiar self. In other words, being completely in the moment makes us fear death because we think that no time means death—we associate the passage of time with life and being alive.

EXPERIENCING NOW-NESS

But remember that you are the presence, the now-ness that is here, and that now-ness is *your* now-ness. You don't need to depart from now-ness to be able to go wherever you are going—in the next minute, or tomorrow afternoon, or wherever you will be after your physical death.

So we are pointing here toward the recognition of the timelessness, or the now-ness, of our True Nature. Presence means that something is in the present, but not just in the sense of being there in present time. Look around you. Whatever you see is in the present—your chair is in the present, your body is in the present, the walls are in the present. But the presence in the present is not just the fact of those things being there, it is the very now-ness of the presence in the present; it is the very experience of now-ness.

How do you experience now? How do you get a taste, a flavor, of now? This flavor, this texture of the now, is the immediacy of the experience of awareness, consciousness, presence. It is like trying to find out what fluid light is made of. It is made out of now, out of nowness. It is an unchanging, condensed now, a full, indestructible now. It is a now that is at all times, for it is the now that is the present of all times—past, present, and future. And it doesn't change from an instant in the past to an instant in the future. It is the same now—always fresh. Time doesn't have an impact on the now.

What is useful to recognize, then, is that our time orientation will disconnect us from our True Nature because it contradicts the now-ness, the timelessness, of our True Nature. It is paradoxical, of course, to think about things that way because we are always thinking in terms of time. The time axis is very important for the mind. The mind is always thinking of things in the past and of what it is going to do in the future. It rarely settles in the moment. If it did, it would become quiet.

When you settle into the moment, you realize that there is not much happening—a few things here and there. The primary aware-ness is of the immediacy of the moment. This is because presence—being in the now—is characterized by beingness, simply being here now. In contrast, our familiar self is based on doing, going, making things happen. We do not trust that action can arise and proceed from inner stillness; we do not recognize that Being is the ground of everything. To be in the now connects you with that quiet beingness that underlies all changes, all activity—the simple hereness where what is most basic is not activity but presence.

So when we are not settled, all the images, all the reifications, all the projections from the past arise and influence the present. We don't see the present as the present; and we don't experience the presence of the present.

MISSING THE NOW-NESS
IN THE PRESENT

That same influence of the past also keeps orienting us toward the future. Something will come up from the past that we are not happy about, and in our desire for things to be better in the future, we dis-connect ourselves from the moment. We miss the now. And when we miss the now, we don't just waste time, we miss the now-ness of what we are, the realness, the here-ness—the very fact that we are.

When people talk about being in the here and now, it is a more profound experience than simply being aware of the content of the experience of the moment. It begins with that awareness because the content of the moment is what is arising now. So, we are aware of the content of the moment—the physical attributes, the feelings, and the thoughts that are arising in the moment. But the more we are attuned to what is arising in the moment, the more time slows down as we become more present to the moment. And when we become more present to the moment, we begin to recognize the now-ness itself, which turns out to be the presence that is present to the moment.

So, my presence is the now-ness of the moment; they are not separate. It is not that my presence is present in the now of the moment; the presence *is* the now of the moment. That is how we actually know what presence is. In the practice of being where we are, it becomes clear that to be ourselves, to be real, we need to be in the present moment. We need to attend to the moment, we need to embrace and be completely aware, immediately in touch, with the moment. This immediate in-touchness with the moment is the in-touchness with the now-ness of the moment, which is the same thing as the Being of our presence.

CAUGHT IN THE FLOW OF TIME

In some sense, all the obstacles to being ourselves that we have observed and explored so far are basically in time; they are a function of the passage of time perceived in the linear sense. They come from the past and move into the future. If our center of consciousness is operating within a linear time framework—in the passage from the past to the future—it will be engaged in these obstacles. Our judgments and rejections and hopes and desires and expectations all happen in time. Even our inner practice becomes a practice in time. We are going from one point of time to another for a process that has a beginning and an end. There is a cause and a result: something we do now will result in a change in the future. That kind of time orientation will dislocate us, will take us outside the presence of what we are and into the ephemeral mental world of time, which is where most people live.

People are living in the bardo—in the passage, in the transitional. That is what the bardo really is: continuous transitioning from one thing to another, which is the product of the experience of a time-bound mind. So, when we say to be present and to be aware of where we are, we simply mean to attend to the moment, to be in the moment, to be here, to be now, to be aware of what is happening right this moment.

Even if I am remembering and reliving something that happened to me in my childhood, I can do that in the moment. In fact, the more I am in the moment, the more real, the more alive, that reliving is. If I relive an incident in my mind, it is more like a thought, a memory; but if I am really in my body, in my sensations, in my presence, in the immediacy, I am in a sense experiencing the now-ness of that past because I am in the now-ness now. But it is the same now-ness.

Remember that light from a distant star is not moving in time; that is, no passage of time is involved in its journey. As we are seeing it, it is the same light that was there billions of years ago. It hasn't aged a minute, even a second. It is always now, and in this now-ness we can experience the past as much as we like—fully, completely— and really process it. Because that is true reliving; it is not just remembering. But we have to be in the moment, we have to be in touch with our presence.

This is one reason the practice of presence is often referred to as *self-remembering*, or simply as remembering. We do not mean remembering in the ordinary, cerebral way that memory usually functions. We mean the remembering of our presence, remembering it in the sense of reliving the presence—which is reliving the now, which is the now of the present moment. In other words, self-remembering works as a practice of presence if and when we can do it in this fullness of being in the now, in the full experience of true reliving.

PAST, FUTURE, AND PRESENCE

Thus far in our considerations, we have seen how our past knowl-edge—what I call learned ignorance—impinges on our experience by mentally overlaying the past on the present. This affects both the central component of our present experience—what we have called the primary manifestation—and the reactions, associations, and judgments about that central component—what we have called the secondary manifestations. If we look at learned ignorance in terms of these two manifestations, we see that the primary component is mainly bound by the past. The secondary components, although controlled by the past, are usually oriented toward accomplishing something or going someplace in the future: "No, I don't like this; I want it that way" or "I like this, and I am going to get it" or "I am afraid that I won't be happy with how this turns out" or "Let's work on this so it will change." All the rejection and the comparison we engage in imply a future orientation, a hope for something different or fear of a bad result. So although primary and secondary manifesta-tions are both involved with past and future, the primary tends to be mostly dominated by the past and the secondary are dominated by the future.

Most commonly, what we identify with is our future orientation. And that is why we keep our attention on the secondary manifesta-tions of our experience. The primary component of our experience often doesn't even have a chance to impact us, much less the actual reality of presence at the heart of it.

Think about it. You still believe that you know there is going to be a tomorrow and that expectation becomes a controlling aspect of your experience. Perhaps you have an appointment tomorrow, so you do need to consider the future in that sense. But that is not the same thing as your consciousness levitating out of the now and jumping to the future.

We don't need to do that in order to be efficient. We can still reside in the present, enjoying the moment—because really, that is all that we have. The future might never come—who knows? So just like anything else that may arise in our experience, we don't have to go along with our future orientation. When we notice it coming up, we don't have to believe it, we don't have to take it seriously, we don't have to identify with it.

But not identifying doesn't mean pushing away. Instead, we can recognize, "Who I truly am is a being of light." When we know this, we don't get caught up in all the obstacles we encounter. Not because we are avoiding them or denying them or pushing them away, but because those obstacles actually don't exist for beings of light. For a being of light, what you are right this very moment is all you have. It is in the presence of this moment, and only in the presence of this moment, that we can be where we are, that we can be ourselves, that we can be real. It is as simple as that.

EXPLORATION SESSION

The Influence of Future Thinking on Your Experience

We have worked a lot so far on the influence of the past, so here the focus is more on your future orientation. This inquiry is to explore the particular way your mind dissociates you from the presence of this moment by looking toward the future.

Be aware that future orientation happens when you engage in any of the following activities: hoping for something, expecting an outcome, fearing that something might happen, planning for the future, having a goal, anticipating accomplishment, or seeking pleasure.

Spend about fifteen minutes observing and following your present experience. Notice what happens to your experience of the present moment. Does a future orientation arise? If so, how does that affect your presence now and how does it affect your experience? What relevance does the future have to yourself as a being of light?

CHAPTER 14

A Mercurial
Sense of Self

AFTER ALL THE EXPLORATIONS you have done thus far of the
obstacles to being who you are and where you are, you may be
feeling more relaxed and content just being yourself. Perhaps you
have succeeded in your practice for some time and are able to let
yourself be more settled and present in the now. After letting go of
some of the strain and effort to be something or to attain a goal, you
might even be experiencing a kind of vacation!

But that state rarely remains for long. Before you know it, it starts
to slip away. Whenever this happens, the tendency is to become
alarmed: "Uh-oh, I've lost it! I have to find where I am again . . . and
it's going to take me a while to find myself." We're right back in time,
and we can easily get caught in trying to preserve where we are, trying to keep everything in place, trying to keep things the same. Even
though we have learned much about not attempting to change ourselves, and we understand better the importance of not trying to

modify our experience, we can end up struggling against change. Why? Because if we like where we are, we want to hold on to it. So what do we need to understand about the nature of reality and about ourselves that will help us with this dilemma?

You can observe through your own experience that the details within manifestation are always moving, always changing, always flowing. In fact, they are quite slippery. The weather changes, who we come in contact with changes, the conditions in the world are always changing, and so on. But not only does our environment change, we ourselves are also in constant change. Simply because we move, for example, our perception changes. And as we know from our experience, our feelings are changing all the time. Thus, our internal and external realities are in a constant state of flux. If you consider this, the question naturally arises: If everything is changing, what does it mean to be where we are?

In this chapter, we want to bring into focus a property of experience that is always there—the fact of change. This constant change is a natural, universal law. All experience and perception imply change. If there is no change, there is simply no experience. The phenomenon of constant change is part of awareness, is part of consciousness, is part of life.

What does that tell us about what it means to be ourselves? What we will discover is that because everything keeps changing and change is a constant, to be where we are means always leaving where we were. This does not mean leaving in the sense of dissociation or becoming disconnected from ourselves, but leaving where we were in order to be with the constantly changing reality of our experience in the moment.

OUR RESISTANCE TO CHANGE

This fact of continuous change discloses something important about what it means to be where we are and also reveals to us a particular obstacle to being where we are. Consider the following example: You have a certain experience and recognize, "I am feeling frustration about this," or "Oh, I'm actually afraid of this." Then you say, "Good—now I know where I am, so I will stay here and explore it." So you do that and have an experience of knowing yourself. But remember the tendency for reification and identification. We almost always reify what we find out about ourselves; we make it into a something and identify with it. And what does identification imply? An attempt to keep things the same.

We have many reasons for trying to keep our experience from changing. We just don't want to lose what we like about what we are experiencing, what we have, what we know about ourselves, or what we take to be reality. When we begin to do inner work, we have a certain view of reality and who we think we are. After some investigation, inquiry, and practice, we form a different view and can learn to abide in that, but there are no guarantees that things are going to stay that way. Our reality changes in so many unexpected ways and directions that the next moment could be, and often is, different.

Change is difficult for the ego. Ego wants stability, sameness. We believe that our sense of self cannot find or keep its mooring if things keep shifting. But the fact is that reality is always a shifting ground. And our consciousness, our awareness, is more like mercury—very slippery, very fluid, easily changing and flowing.

So when we talk about remaining where we are, it does not mean that we remain static; it implies being at ease with the continual transformation of where we are. Our tendency is to want to stay the same and have our experience remain the same, especially when we like it. And that becomes a rigidity in our consciousness, an inflexibility that is not natural. How can we approach this situation and understand what is at work here?

THE ATTEMPT TO PRESERVE

We have looked at many of the ways we try to change our experience to improve it, to make it better, or to direct it toward a particular goal. Our attempt to change things to be a certain way is a primary obstacle to just being where we are. But the opposite is also true. The attempt to preserve is as much an obstacle to being where we are as the attempt to change.

Each time we try to change something in our experience, we are also trying to preserve something else. For instance, whenever we are trying to improve our experience, we are preserving a certain ideal or goal. By shaping our experience to be a particular way instead of letting it unfold the way it wants to, we are really trying to maintain a certain image of ourselves, an identity that we don't want to change.

Let's say that a business partner you trusted just cheated you out of a lot of money. If you carry an ideal of being a forgiving person, you probably will make it a goal to forgive your partner. But what if your immediate reaction is anger and hurt, and you are not ready or don't want to forgive that person? If you force yourself to do it without being with the experiences that are arising in you, you are not being where you are or who you are; you are trying to hold on to a self-image that is not you at this moment. It is true that you could reach a point where forgiveness is authentic, but you don't need goals and ideals for that to happen. In fact, the insistence on maintaining the self-image of being a forgiving person is likely to delay or maybe even block the natural resolution of your feelings. If your True Nature includes forgiveness, eventually that is what will arise, on its own, when the issues and feelings around the incident are faced consciously.

So we can put the brakes on and resist change, or we can try to direct it, and we probably do both things at different times. But we don't have to fight with that or try to change that. We can just recognize our attachment and see how we are holding on to things so that they don't change. That is all we need to know, because experience changes on its own. The practice, then, is once again to see where we are and be there. So everything we find ourselves doing— even our attempts to change or stay the same—is included in that. Everything is welcomed.

PRESERVING OUR IDENTITY

We can divide into two types the human tendency to hold on to the present in order to stay the same. The first type is the ego manifestation of trying to preserve a posture and identity. The second type is identification with and attachment to particular experiences. We will discuss each of these in some detail.

In the first type, we might find ourselves in a situation where we want to feel better, or we might want our experience to feel freer and more positive—but that doesn't mean we want to change who we are. We still want to preserve our identity as we know it. And even if we believe that we are open to our identity and our character structure changing, forces within us are trying to keep them the same.

So ego experience inherently implies rigidity because we are identified with inner structures that are already defined and packaged. The fact that we are identifying with a self-image or an impression of ourselves or a pattern from the past means that we are repeating the same thing. We are not allowing space, we are not open for something different to arise. By holding on to that particular image, pattern, or way of relating, we are obstructing our own movement and unfoldment.

We recognize that we are a certain kind of a person or that we are in a certain condition. And we notice that even when we want to change, even when we want to grow or we want to learn, it is not easy. We discover an inflexibility in our experience, a rigid boundary about what can and cannot change. Sometimes we can see that our experience is always changing, and we know that our body is changing and growing. But if we are honest, we have to admit that, in the midst of that change, we are always trying to hold on to something constant. We keep thinking more or less in the same way; even though our particular thoughts change from minute to minute, our repertoire is limited, and what we think about repeats over and over and over again.

Everybody else would have been bored silly by now if they had to watch that same movie thousands of times. But we don't get bored with it! The scenes have become our reality; they are what we are—and if the movie starts to change, alarms go off. We don't want something different. We don't even want a sequel! In fact, seeing the plot and the characters the same way so many times makes us feel secure. "Oh, this scene is happening again . . . yes, this is me . . . I recognize myself." You are on familiar ground. The same issues arise—you feel hurt, or rejected, or small. You don't like it, you complain about it, and go to therapy to work on it. But if one of these days you woke up without it, you would freak out. Who would you be then?

It is as though we cannot exist without those unchanging parts of our experience or sense of self. And the inner activity, the inner posture, of holding on to that sense of who we are becomes an inflexibility, a rigidity. Other people can recognize that kind of rigidity in you, especially if it shows up as a characteristic or habit they don't like. For example, if you are always late, friends may talk to you about it and want you to change. But, in many cases, it doesn't change and you continue to be late. In fact, if you started being on time, it would be as though you had turned into somebody else.

When the ego defines everything about who we are, we don't have our hands off the situations of our lives; it is more like our hands are gripping them, holding them in a fixed position so they can't change.

Many of us cannot envision the possibility that our identity can actually change. It seems impossible to us that our experience can be so different that the person we have known ourselves to be becomes like a stranger. Can you imagine not even being able to relate to that person, finding it difficult to remember who you were—or how you used to feel?

It is possible.

A point does come during the inner journey when our transformation is so profound that we are unrecognizable to ourselves. It's not that we don't recognize what is happening; it's that we realize that what is happening is not familiar. This can be disconcerting, but it is also freeing. We are no longer an extension of how we felt, what we did, how we behaved. Sometimes the change is so fundamental that we don't just feel like a different person—we don't remember our-

selves as a person at all! We experience ourselves as just a mass of
light that has taken the shape of a person for a while. There is an
indescribable freedom when you can say, "I recognize my original
nature . . . this timeless light."

But most of us are not able to go beyond our ego rigidity, which is
an identification with and an attachment to the usual forms—our
expressions of character, our types of experiencing, and the kinds of
experience and capacities we have. That identification creates a lack
of openness to the moment, because the moment can be anything
and it can bring anything. Each moment is. The moment it has happened, it is gone, and another moment arises that might be similar—
or it might be entirely different.

So what is freedom? Freedom is, "I know that whatever happens
in each moment is, and always will be, fine." We are comfortable
with whatever is, because we don't have a rigid sense of what we are,
who we are, what kind of experience is supposed to happen, or what
is possible.

What can we recognize, then, about our ego-created sense of self
that limits our freedom to be ourselves and to live truly in the
moment? The following is a list of things we know about our identity,
which we are so attached to preserving:

- The ego sets structures in place that need to continue as they are
  so we can maintain our identity.
- We have always depended on our ego for our general sense of
  identity and self-image and for self-recognition, orientation,
  familiarity, and knowing how to function in the world.
- Our ego-created identity is an implicit constancy that we have
  become accustomed to.
- We think we need this identity to know who we are, to feel on
  familiar ground, to feel secure.
- This identity defines the ways we generally think and feel and
  includes momentary states that we identify with in a particular
  way, such as occasional flare-ups of anger that we feel guilty about
  afterward.

- Though we grow and transform in many ways, the basics that comprise our ego identity—how we think about things, our range of moods, how we do things, our preferences, the kinds of relationships and projections we have, and so on—tend not to fundamentally change.

- Even when we have significant realizations and insights, we tend to come back to the home base of who we take ourselves to be. Our identity coalesces back into the sameness of what we already know. And our experiences of realization become just little trips we have taken, rather than bringing a fundamental change in identity.

ATTACHMENT

The second category of resistance to change is our attachment to our experiences. We can identify with any kind of experience, but we tend to get most attached to new experiences that we find pleasurable or freeing. Identifying with an experience means that we don't want it to go away. We like it the way it is and will be disappointed if it changes to something else; we will feel it as a sense of loss. So we engage in subtle, or not so subtle, holding on—getting glued to the experience, trying to nail it down, trying to stop the unfolding of the moment in order to keep things as they are. Even when we are more open, even when we are experiencing our True Nature, we are not freed yet, we are not secure in the dynamic freedom inherent in being what we truly are.

At the beginning of our journey, our experience is always changing, even when we are not in contact with presence or aware of Being. It is changing from one feeling to another, from one emotional state to another, from one thought to another, from one self-image to another, from one reaction to another. And when we explore our experience, inquire into it to become more present, that doesn't mean our experience can or will stay still. We may slow it down to become more aware of it, but it will change.

When we are further along in our practice and have experience of and contact with essential presence, we discover the natural dynamism of Being as that presence constantly changes as well. It might be a spaciousness one moment, and the next moment it could be pregnant light . . . then a flowing river . . . then a solid sense of presence . . . then a galactic condition. And all the while, there may be ego reactions around the presence that are also changing, such as fear, hope, resistance, or possessiveness.

If we get to a point where we finally experience our essential worth and feel the solidity and steadfastness of it, we might get attached to that because we like it—it is new, and we are excited about it. We also can fall into expecting it to continue or wishing or hoping it will. However, if it continues in the same way, our learning will stop, our maturation will stop. True Nature does not remain in place like that; it is constantly disclosing, displaying its possibilities. It's always revealing itself in other forms, deeper forms, subtler forms, more comprehensive forms.

Even when we get to the nondual condition where everything is presence, nothing about that is static. Yes, it is always presence, but everything is flowing and unfolding, and that presence can be of so many colors and flavors. Presence sometimes becomes denser, sometimes lighter. And sometimes, the presence is not like presence at all but more of a nothingness or an absence. Our soul needs to have completely slippery hands so she is prevented from holding on to anything. Velcro is not a condition of realization!

PRESERVING OUR CONCEPT OF TIME

It is useful to notice how our attempts to preserve what we like and to change what we don't like are generally wrapped up in our concept of time. All our concepts of change tend to be time bound. Why? Because time indicates change; it is basically a measurement of change. So if we are focused on creating change or on resisting change, we will be operating in time. We will be experiencing moving forward in time: going somewhere or trying not to go there. But we are not really going anywhere. The feeling that we are going someplace is always an illusion. It is just a way of experiencing things. In fact, all that is happening is that experience is changing.

How can we understand this? As we discovered in the last chapter, time slows down the more we are being presence. When we are fully present in the presence, there is no time—no time passes. What does that mean in terms of our experience? Expressing this experience as "I am in timelessness, in the now; no time is passing for me" implies a still frame in which I am not moving. Does this mean that our experience doesn't change? Does it mean that we don't really have experiences and are just an unchanging blankness?

These are common questions that arise when we start to explore the implications of timeless presence. We think that way because we cannot imagine how change can happen without the passage of time. It is as though time were a larger concept, a larger reality, within which things happen. In that schema, movement in space also means movement in time. If you go from one end of the room to the other, time will pass as that happens. This is how we experience and conceive of movement and change—as something that requires time to occur. So how could change be perceived without the passage of time? To answer this, we need to understand more about our True Nature as the presence of ever-fresh light.

When I am my True Nature as a being of light, I am like a field, a presence, an effulgence. This doesn't mean that I am like the steady bright light we experience coming from the sun. Our True Nature is not just a medium of light, a transparent, luminous presence. It is magical light—light that continues to be a light but is always changing. It changes its color, its shape, its density, its texture. It can actually take on the forms of emotions, thoughts, images, and sensations. This light that I am is always forming itself into one thing or another. And this forming itself into one thing or another I recognize as the various experiences that I have.

If the light is sometimes a white light and sometimes a green light, we might think this means that first it was white and then it became green and therefore some time must have passed. But if we are *in* the light, if we *are* the light, the change from white to green is not from the past to the future. Transformation does not occur in a progression from the past to the present to the future, which is how we usually think of it and experience it.

The change, instead, is more of an outflow: The forms just appear, they arise out of nowhere. The source of our experience is not the past as our mind understands it, but some mysterious immediacy of the moment. So the movement is from no form to the presence of form, from nothing to something, and it is instantaneous. Our eyes see a constancy of forms, but our actual experience is of an ever-fresh arising of those forms in an unfolding now. And perceived changes are simply the patterns in the outflowing of the forms.

When we experience things as an outflow in this way—as consciousness continuously flowing out and bringing forth different forms of experience—then the sense of time is gone. There is no awareness of time passing. We feel that we are in the now, but the now is always manifesting itself in different ways. It is in constant transformation, even though it is the same. It is always the now and it is clearly the presence of the now, the constantly renewing light of True Nature. It is the timeless moment that is always transforming its form.

When we don't recognize light as being the medium, we just see the objects that arise. And when we see forms and notice that they change, we immediately bring in something we call time to account for the change. We say that something happened and then something else happened, and we see it as a series of events that is taking place in time. However, this is a substitute for recognizing how things actually happen, how things are constantly being displayed, how the light is always changing itself into various forms. And in that substitution, we miss the fact that this light, this awareness, this consciousness, pervades with immediacy all the forms and is aware of them.

It is the nature of our True Nature to be not only a presence but a dynamic presence, a dynamism that is always disclosing its potential, revealing all the forms it can possibly be. True Nature is not a monolithic presence that stays the same; it is constantly transforming, always responding to what is going on. And it always continues to be True Nature.

Sometimes we experience ourselves in a dimension of True Nature that is unchanging. But even though the ground of True Nature is unchanging, that ground is not separate from all that manifests in it, and all of those manifestations are constantly changing. True Nature is rich with possibilities; its potential is immense and it never ceases to disclose its treasures. It is always revealing its potential, displaying all the forms possible.

We are learning here about the relationship of True Nature to the various manifestations. Part of our ignorance is in not understanding clearly what the relationship of True Nature is to everything else. Everything else is just a form that True Nature takes. Or you could say that True Nature manifests itself in its various forms. But it is still True Nature. So although it is always changing in its manifestations, *we* are not being something else. We are being ourselves. The ego creates a sense of being oneself as a fixed, unchanging self. True Nature doesn't need that kind of stability.

So even though we try to hold on to a particular form or a particular way of experiencing, ultimately it is not possible. When we do this, we are trying to stop the dynamism. We are trying to keep that fluid, slippery presence confined in a particular box, stopping it from being dynamic and doing its thing. In doing that, we disconnect from ourselves.

To be where we are, then, we need to recognize the changeable, slippery, transforming, morphing quality of our Being and of reality. That means we have to recognize our attachments, our identifications, the ways we try to hold on, which requires appreciating what we have taken to be permanent features of reality. Have you ever thought about what things you believe to be permanent? For example, don't you think that you are always going to be you? Almost everyone believes, "I can change, but it is always going to be me who is experiencing those changes." We can't imagine waking up one morning and discovering that somebody else is experiencing them!

But if, instead of our usual self, we experience pure awareness as that which is experiencing things, it feels as though it is not us. That's because we have been accustomed to experiencing everything through our usual self-identity. But now it is just experience happening without that usual self; it is just the light, and because that light is luminous, it is aware of what is happening.

Recognizing this, we finally shed that which has always possessed us—we throw it off. We have been exorcised. We are freed from something that was imposed on us, that got into us and took over, that we introjected and identified with and thought was who we were. Now we are no longer identifying with anything; we are being ourselves.

Being ourselves means not holding on to ourselves. Because Being doesn't need to hold on to itself. It *is* itself. Since it is itself and knows that it is itself—without thinking about it or doing anything to keep it that way—it is not concerned with holding on or grasping or attaching or hoping or expecting that it, or any particular experience, will come or leave or stay.

When we are our True Nature, the fact that we don't know whether the next moment will be the same or not is no longer something to contend with. We are completely unconcerned about whether it is going to be the same or not. We have no need to hold on to the past or to get attached to the fresh and new. We recognize that whatever arises in each moment in the play of light in all its luminous forms is none of our business. We become a dynamic flowing, free presence. And that is true freedom.

EXPLORATION SESSION

Exploring Beliefs about Not Changing

In this exercise, you will have the opportunity to explore your experiences and your beliefs about what doesn't change in yourself. The objective is not so much to evaluate the correctness of your perceptions but to allow the whole range of your beliefs, attitudes, and positions to be revealed.

Begin by making a list of things about yourself that don't change. Don't get involved in the distinction in your mind about whether certain things can change or not. The important thing is to see the part of your experience that stays constant and unchanging for whatever reason. When you have finished, take a moment to look over your list.

Next, explore your beliefs and assumptions about what is unchangeable in your experience. Consider these questions: What benefit do you get from having things that don't change? How does it serve you or support you? What do you believe would happen if everything were fluid and nothing in your experience remained fixed, stable, or unchanging? What do you believe is keeping the unchanging elements in place? Don't assume it's your genes or God or fate. Maybe it is one of those, or something else—this is a chance to find out for yourself.

CHAPTER 15

The Personal Thread
of Meaning

IF YOU CONSIDER THE NATURE of your own experience in the light of all we have discussed so far, you can notice certain things: That your experience is always changing. That your perceptions are always changing. That where you are is always changing. It becomes clear at a certain point in our practice that our consciousness is manifesting itself as constant change and transformation. It moves from one kind of feeling or thought or reaction to another, from one kind of state to another.

But have you noticed that it is never a disconnected succession? As long as we are awake, our experience is continuous. It is always a flow of experience. It's not that we have one particular experience and then there is a gap followed by another experience and then another gap.

There are no gaps, really. Our experience is a seamless flow. Even when we go through a transition from one dimension of experience to another, it's still a flow. Because it is really the same consciousness that is constantly unfolding, constantly transforming. That's why our experience is often likened to a stream or a river.

So "being where we are" does not mean finding where we are and staying there and that's it. Being where we are is a continuous practice in the sense that as we continue to be where we are, where we are changes and transforms. Thus, being ourselves, being who we are, being where we are, becomes a continuity of being—the flow of being.

FLOW OF EXPERIENCE

We're usually not aware of the continuity of our experience. We know that there is continuity because our ongoing experience has no gaps in it. But we're not usually aware of the continuity of the forms that experience takes—how one form transforms to another or makes space for another in a meaningful way. In other words, we are not present at each moment to directly experience the continuity.

To truly be where we are combines having the awareness of where we are, being the presence of where we are, and understanding the truth of where we are. When we bring those three elements together, being where we are becomes a practice that is necessary to become aware of the flow of being. You see, we are always someplace—one way or another, we are where we are—but we're usually not aware of what that place is. We don't get it; we don't see it. Our attention, our awareness is scattered and distracted, involved with all kinds of peripheral, secondary manifestations.

However, once we can focus and recognize our primary manifestation, we locate ourselves. And, if we pay attention, we find that the primary manifestation of where we are continuously changes—it is a continuity, a flow. It is not static.

CONTINUITY THROUGHOUT
THE STAGES

Looking at the three stages of development as we have described them in this book can help us better understand this continuity of being where we are. When we see what the continuity of being ourselves means at each stage, what we discover is that it is also the continuity of meaning, not just of experience.

In the first stage, to be where we are means recognizing where we are and understanding where we are. We not only have the awareness and feeling of what is happening, but we also know what it's about and why it is happening. We know in a way that is meaningful—in other words, in a way that makes sense of our experience. And if we're really practicing, if we're continuing to inquire, to be aware, to be present, then our experience becomes a continuity of meaning, not just a series of events and states strung together. As our experience flows and transforms, it's a meaningful flow, a meaningful transformation.

For example, maybe you become aware of a particular feeling, and you recognize, "Oh, I'm feeling this sadness because of that event . . . and now this is happening . . . and now I see how it relates to what happened before, and why I felt that then and am feeling this other feeling now." The continuum of experience makes sense to you. It's meaningful.

When we're not practicing, when we're not aware of where we are, our experience does not have that kind of meaning. It seems disconnected: "I did this and I did that, and this happened and I felt that." We don't know how all of these events relate, because we are not really there. We are not being where we are, so the continuity of meaning is not present.

When we go on to the second stage—the journey with presence—the meaning becomes clear as being the presence itself. We understand our experience at this stage by being the presence that we are and discovering how it threads together the various manifestations—

feelings, ideas, reactions, behaviors—in our life. Thus, the capacity to experience the centrality of Being in its various qualities deepens the first-stage level of understanding, moving us to the second.

When we arrive at the third stage, the meaning of our experience continues to be the presence, but now everything else is inseparable from that presence, so all manifestation is imbued with the meaningfulness of presence. And that meaning is the recognition, the comprehension, the direct knowing of what reality is—how it appears, how it works, and how it is manifesting at this moment, in this situation. The primary meaning is the omnipresent presence itself, and the secondary meaning is the understanding of the manifestations that this presence is displaying.

THE PERSONAL THREAD

So as you see, there is always a continuity of meaning for each of us, if we're really practicing being where we are. This continuity of meaning I call the personal thread. A lot is happening in the universe. The universe itself is flowing and moving and changing, and everybody and everything that composes it is moving and changing as well. Within that shared reality, each one of us is having our own personal experience in terms of where we are—our personal thread. Recognizing our personal experience, being with it, feeling it with immediacy and awareness and understanding—brings not only meaning but a thread of meaning, a continuity of meaning. And this thread of meaning is our own individual unfolding journey of truth.

The significance of an individual life arises from this thread of meaning. Our practice of being where we are supports our lives becoming centered on our own personal thread. It becomes the core and the center of our life, because it is the core and center of our awareness, of our experience, of our being here. When we're inquiring, when we're practicing, what we're doing is finding our personal thread, recognizing where it happens to be, and following it.

In Einstein's relativistic geometry, plotting a sequence of points creates what is called a lifeline—the mathematical equivalent of what we have called here our personal thread. In the physical universe, there are four dimensions: three in space and one in time. Within this universe of space-time, every particle has a lifeline—it has a curve or a line that traces where a particle is and has been at each moment. At each instant, that particle is in a certain place, and you could plot its progression in time and space by drawing the line or curve that connects all the specific instants.

Of course, our experiential universe has many more dimensions than just four: the spatial dimension, the time dimension, the feeling dimension, the knowing dimension, the thinking dimension, the color dimension, the sound dimension, the taste dimension, the kinesthetic dimension, the texture dimension, the viscosity dimension, the density dimension, the presence dimension, and so on. All these are dimensions of experience, and we can locate ourselves in each of these dimensions at any given moment. So at each point, at each instant, where we are can be described as a particular intersection point of all these dimensions. This would be where we are in the experiential universe.

THE LIFELINE

What this means is that our life creates a curve within the experiential universe. If you plot all the points of individual experience, you see that everybody has his or her own curve, or lifeline. This lifeline or personal thread is the continuity of our constantly changing experience, the continuity of where we are.

To be where we are means following our lifeline. And when we're practicing, when we are being where we are, when we are not interfering with our experience and just allowing it to happen, our "location" not only moves from one point to another in the experiential universe, but it unfolds and manifests new possibilities.

Sometimes our lifeline manifests new dimensions—dimensions of presence, dimensions of awareness, dimensions of emptiness, dimensions of love—that were not present to us before. And even the feeling or thinking dimensions can unfold possibilities we haven't seen yet. For example, sometimes a deep sadness feels like it's a million miles deep, as though our heart is going to the center of the universe. It doesn't start at that depth, of course, but as we stay where we are and don't resist that feeling, don't try to constrain it, don't stop it from changing, the dynamism of our own Being becomes a disclosure, a revelation of that kind of depth in the dimension of feeling.

So you can look at all of your life as an unfolding thread in the experiential universe, a thread that moves within many dimensions simultaneously. And we are all related threads—sometimes interconnecting, sometimes intersecting—within the universe of experience. But none of that make sense if we're not aware of our experience, if we're not present in it, if we don't have some kind of understanding or recognition of what it is, of its meaning. Remember that this is an unfolding thread of meaning as well as of experience.

And even the word "meaning" changes meaning, as we have seen. It becomes deeper. At the beginning of our journey, maybe meaning is an intellectual meaning; then it becomes more of a felt, emotional meaningfulness; and after that an essential meaning. This continues until it becomes a pure presence, a pure awareness that is meaningful.

THE MEANING OF LIFE

As human beings, we ask, "What is the meaning of life?" From the perspective of the spiritual journey, the answer can only come from where we are. Thus the meaning of life is revealed in the unfolding thread of each person. Because of that, the meaning changes as each of us moves through life. If you ask yourself, "What was the meaning of my life ten years ago?" you can easily recognize that what it was then is different from what it is now. Did it make a quantum jump? It might feel that way, but in fact, the meaning has been continuous. Even when there are quantum jumps in our experience, they still follow Einsteinian law, which is based on continuity.

Einstein believed that the notion of quantum jumps is just an approximation of what happens. We assume quantum changes because we're not paying close enough attention, and our theories are not precise enough, to see the continuity of change. Reality is actually a seamless, self-existing field. We say that it is light, but this light is not composed of particles. It's a fluid that is not particularized; it is constantly flowing and unfolding. That is how reality is all the time.

Why don't we recognize our experience in that way? Because we're not being real, we're not being ourselves. We are not where we are. We're not present where we are. The more we are present where we are, the greater the sense of flow, the sense that there is a meaning to our experience, that a continuum, an unfolding, is at play. So our life becomes meaningful because not only are we in touch with the meaning of our life, we are *being* the meaning of our life. We are at the place where this meaning is unfolding.

Sometimes there might be gaps in your understanding of your experience that you haven't even noticed. When you recognize one, that in itself begins the process of understanding. If we don't recognize that there is a gap, we would believe in a continuity that isn't real. Even to identify a gap before you understand what it is about is immensely helpful.

Through personal inquiry, perhaps the gap will be filled in, and perhaps not. So the meaning might include times of not knowing, times of emptiness or blankness. And as we inquire into that emptiness or blankness, at some point it becomes meaningful and helps us understand the whole picture. We discover that our personal thread wasn't cut—it just was invisible for a while.

EXPLORATION SESSION

Considering Your Own Lifeline

One of the most powerful potentials of the practice of inquiry is the revelation of our personal thread. Consider your experience in the past week. Can you identify what your unfolding thread has been?

To do this you need to revisit where you have been—what you know about where you were at various points during the week.

Include as much as you can about what you were experiencing physically, mentally, and emotionally. Identify the secondary and primary manifestations you were aware of in yourself. Reflect on what you can see about the deeper nature of what was happening.

As you consider these various moments in time, can you see a flow or a progression between them? What do you understand about how these various experiences might be related? Do you find a thread of meaning? Can you also see the gaps where you have no sense of what connects one experience with another?

Continue your exploration all the way to the present moment. The thread is there, but you may not be able to recognize it yet. It is not something you can figure out with your mind. Do not be discouraged if this continuity of your soul's subtle unfoldment is not apparent. Simply opening yourself to the possibility will make more space for it to make itself known.

CHAPTER 16

Being without Mind

As we become more and more attuned to what is happening in our experience, our capacity to understand ourselves at increasingly subtler levels continues to develop. The more we continue to recognize and work with the different primary and secondary elements of our experience that we have discussed so far, the more we feel what it is like to be where we are, to be ourselves.

However, this capacity to know and be who we are is not based on what we understand conceptually about manifestations and how they all fit together. Being ourselves is not the outcome of mentally arranging all the pieces of a puzzle correctly to get the complete picture. It arises—or you could say it is evoked—by seeing through the beliefs we have about who we are and letting go of all the ways we stop ourselves from being who we are. And as this being who we are is revealed, we simultaneously come to know it directly without relying on our mind. In this chapter, we will be exploring a new dimension of Being that is the ground for this nonconceptual self-knowing.

We have been working with the practice of nondoing by learning how to be where we are without doing anything to be where we are.

We have seen how by simply being aware, we are able to recognize at some point what is happening in our experience, to understand it, see the meaning of it. We have seen that this meaning over time becomes a thread of meaning, our personal thread, which transforms into essential meaning, which is the presence of True Nature itself.

We have seen how our mind recognizes our experience, reifies it, and then identifies with those reifications. We have explored how the reification process makes objects out of the elements in our experience and how, through identification, our mind constrains the flow of that experience. And we have noticed how our mind blocks the natural unfoldment of our experience by attempting to hold on to some parts of it and reject or change others, thus creating a fixed sense of self.

If we were left with only this situation, the outlook would be bleak. Who would be able to avoid the pitfalls of reification and identification? The mind engages in these activities naturally, easily, and almost instantaneously after each experience. As a result, they are so second nature to us that it is difficult to recognize that they are even going on.

As we look closer at these subtle ego activities, we discover the tendency to reify reification itself and make it a kind of object to reject. In our minds, we make it something from which we can push away and separate ourselves.

The same process can happen as we reify doing, making it something to reject or judge. Even more subtle than that—we can reify nondoing, such that nondoing becomes an object, a thing we can value or cultivate. The truth is that nondoing is really nothing. No such thing exists that is called nondoing. Nondoing is the nonexistence of doing, but we make it something to aspire to, which can become a subtle obstacle. Something similar can happen to those who work exclusively with a nondual perspective about reality: at some point, they begin to reify nonduality, and it becomes for them an objective to aspire to and reach.

So, as you see, the tendency of the mind to reify in order to create stability, a fixed center, or a particular orientation is unlimited. The mind, then, is a mixed blessing, a double-edged sword. And that is the condition of humanity: Our intelligence, our mind, can liberate us but it can also ensnare us. Our learning, our maturation, and even our realization and enlightenment, require the capacity for discernment, for clear discrimination, of what is true and what is not true. But it is this capacity for discernment that also becomes the basis for reification. Reification cannot begin without the recognition of something, without discriminating it as distinct from everything else.

When we recognize something, we usually encapsulate it, we make it into an object, reify it, remember it, and then project it onto the present—all of which excludes the immediacy of our experience. We are, as a result, perceiving our experience through the reifications. No longer are we recognizing reality freshly. When we first recognize something—before the reification happens—the recognition is immediate. It is a felt, full sense of experiential knowing of what is. This immediate discernment is alive and unmediated by past experience. Meeting reality in this way is necessary in order to be a full human being; without it, our potentialities will become limited. We will continue to perceive our experience based on a reified reality that cuts us off from the direct knowing of life.

But it is actually possible not to get ensnared in reification and identification and all the things that go along with them, such as judgment, rejection, hatred, division, and attachment. What makes this possible? True Nature itself. Because True Nature is what is—it is reality and it is independent of the mind. Whether we reify it or not, True Nature is itself. We may reify it, and thereby distance ourselves from it, but nothing alters it from what it is. Nothing ever happens to it.

PERCEPTUAL VERSUS COGNITIVE AWARENESS

So True Nature is beyond mind. And it is the facet beyond mind, a dimension we have not yet explored, that allows us not to get caught in the conceptual trap of learned ignorance.

When we were discussing the different kinds of ignorance earlier in this book, we saw that at the beginning of our development as human beings, our conceptual knowingness—which we also call our cognitive capacity or our discriminating ability—is rudimentary, almost nonexistent. It develops gradually until we are able to recognize concrete objects, and then we are able to move into more abstract activity—into thinking and mental conceptualization. But even before we have that cognitive capacity, True Nature has an awareness. Animals have awareness, and it is that awareness that causes them to respond. And the fact that we human beings have awareness even as infants tells us that True Nature has a capacity to be aware that is more fundamental than our capacity to know.

This capacity is what I call perceptual, or pure, awareness, in contrast to knowing awareness or cognitive awareness. From the time we are born, we perceive. We might not know that we perceive, but we definitely have perception. We don't have the cognitive awareness that develops later, but we have the perceptual awareness.

As the cognitive components of awareness develop, some beginning quite early in life, we gradually lose touch with or forget about the purely perceptual awareness. We get accustomed to our awareness always being a knowing awareness, a cognitive awareness. You see an object and either you know what it is or you don't. If you have never seen a light bulb and then you come across one, you recognize that something is there, but you know that you don't know what it is—you don't have a name for it—because you have never seen one. This is different from the perception of a human infant or a bird that sees that same light bulb; it sees the bulb, and it doesn't know what it is either, but it doesn't *know* that it doesn't know what it is.

As human beings, we have the capacity to perceive without knowing and that is never lost. This capacity is the ground of cognitive knowing, because our knowing awareness developed as a facet of our original consciousness, our primordial awareness. But as the cognitive capacity develops its reifying capacity, we lose touch with the pure, perceptual awareness—the sensitivity itself without the cognitive knowing. We don't know it exists because the perception and the knowing seem to happen at the same time, and we can't separate them. We perceive something and right away our cognitive capacity registers that we either know or we don't know what it is.

Actually, it seems to us that perception and knowing occur simultaneously, but the fact is that first we perceive, and knowledge about what we perceive follows. When we see somebody walking, it registers as either "I know this person" or "I don't know this person." You don't see somebody and immediately think, "What is that?" You at least know, because of your cognitive capacity, that it is a person. We don't have the kind of baby mind that can see something and perceive it with a complete freshness and immediacy. Actually we do have that kind of mind, but it has been obscured, absorbed into the knowing mind.

So, we cannot know without perception, and we have become accustomed to the belief that knowing is always part of perception. But if that were the case, what happened to the kind of perception we had before we were able to recognize what things are? We have become so used to the dominance of our cognitive capacity that we may not even realize that True Nature inherently has a perceptual awareness independent of cognitive knowing. Our knowing, our cognitive capacity, develops and matures through our human experience, and yet we actually do not lose the original pure awareness. It simply becomes invisible to us, for we are almost always perceiving through the window of knowing.

BEYOND DISCRIMINATION

How do these understandings relate to our practice of inquiry? In the inner investigation we do while just sitting—not engaging the content of the mind and not going along with its reactions—we begin at some point to recognize certain tendencies. We see our tendency to recognize things in our experience and to want to know what they are. We see our tendency to want to label everything: "Is this a feeling or a thought? Is this feeling anger or anxiety? Is it a pain in the butt, a projection, a suppressed memory, a revelation of essential truth?" At the beginning of the journey of inquiry, those kinds of questions are useful, as we know, because they help us to be aware of things we might not have known were there. And that is why some meditation practices suggest that you label the content of your experience: because labeling can clarify what is there.

But the labeling also becomes the ground upon which reification can be built and regardless of how smart and aware you are, your mind works so fast that it will reify things before you are aware of it. Before you know it, you are encapsulated in the reification. It's as though you had been shrink-wrapped by one of those machines that seal up objects. You are sitting there wrapped in cellophane that has a label with your name on it! Labeling is only useful in clarifying our experience up to a point because it is so closely linked with reification and objectification.

As we begin to recognize how knowing and labeling can both help and entrap us, we can experience the underlying ground of more immediate and direct knowing, which occurs prior to labeling and reification. Our knowingness can shift from the discursive kind of reified knowing into a more immediate knowing in which we recognize that knowingness is part of what we are. If we become more secure in this implicit knowingness, we don't need to name things because the knowingness is inherent by now; the cognitive potential of the awareness has been actualized.

In other words, we can move, by following the thread of our meaning, from the normal knowing, which is mediated and representational, to the immediate knowing of presence, where knowing and being are the same thing. This is what is traditionally known as gnosis—knowing by being what we know. When we are secure in this more basic level of knowing, we feel relaxed about knowing. We feel that we do not need to hold on to knowing in order to be ourselves, for knowing is part of our inherent potential, a facet of our being. Then it becomes possible to relax to the point where the knowing capacity itself dissolves.

It is not only the labeling that becomes unnecessary; the recognition itself at some point might not be necessary—at least not always. After sitting and meditating for a while, when we are quiet, in presence and in clarity, there is no need to label and no need to know anything in particular. We can be in a place where we don't recognize anything in particular, but still we have clarity, we have bright, clear, transparent awareness. It is very crisp, very sharp and clean, without our focusing on anything in particular or defining, "This is this" or "This is that." We go back to our original, primordial condition before the cognitive capacity developed and took over.

But it is not a going back in time, it is a "going back" ontologically, in the moment, in the sense that we have let go of one layer and now are perceiving from the underlying layer of perceptual awareness. And that layer has been and always is there; otherwise we could not perceive.

PURE AWARENESS

We can eventually become quiet enough or secure enough in our knowingness that we no longer need to hold on to our knowing. Or perhaps through our inquiring, we have come to recognize what knowingness can and cannot do—we have seen its capacity completely, and so we don't need to reify the knowing as something to hold on to. Either way, something falls off. The need to hold on to that knowing falls away, and there is just the luminosity of Being, on its own. And our True Nature continues to be our True Nature— because it is timeless, eternal. It was there before we started to know and it continues to be there.

Through our experience of living, we have developed the potential of True Nature to know, but True Nature is itself beyond that; it is pre-knowing, more primordial than knowing. It is just the "simply being there"—the awareness of being there without the awareness of being there meaning anything. The experience is: "I am aware of being here, but there is nothing in the mind that says I am aware of being here. There is no recognition of being here; I am just being here."

Sometimes you see this in babies who are looking at you in a certain way. They are very present, but you can tell that they are not reflecting on themselves; they are not thinking that they are being there or that they are looking at you. Although they have a very present, focused attention, there is no thinking about themselves or recognizing anything—only bare awareness. When that happens, there is no responding, no reacting on their part; they are just there perceiving. And that happens usually when they are in a state of relaxation or satisfaction. The same is true with animals. When they are satisfied or relaxed, and no threat is present, there is just the bare awareness of and sensitivity to, what is.

These observations show us that the capacity of pure perception is a potential of our True Nature. Our True Nature has in it this dimension of pure awareness, which is actually presence. But usually presence has a cognitive capacity; it knows that it is. What we are talking about here is a presence that doesn't know that it is—just as it operates in a baby. In that state, you don't experience the fact of not knowing as a feeling of something missing. What you recognize is: "I am complete. I am so much myself that I don't need to know. Anyway, I already know True Nature, so why do I have to think about it? I know it, and it is me—continuously. I understand that the mind has done its job. It has brought me to the place where I can recognize True Nature and see it for what it is. And now I can sit in it with confidence and know that it is not something I can lose—or gain."

You are so relaxed that you don't even think about it. That kind of presence is natural—"first nature," not even second nature. And it comes with a sense of innocence, the fresh awareness that reveals everything as though you were seeing it for the first time. Whenever we know what something is, we can associate it with another time when we saw the same thing. But if we look at it with pure awareness, it is as though we had never seen it before. It is fresh and new—everything is glistening, just being born. Everything is clean, transparent, light, crisp—it is just as it is—because the mind is not doing anything to it. And the mind is not doing anything because it is simply not there. Mind enters with knowing, but this is before knowing, when there is just pure perception.

BEYOND THE DISCERNING MIND

At some point in the development of our capacity to discern, the cognitive capacity can take itself to its own limits. And that is really what the inner work is about: taking the discerning capacity to its ultimate limit, where reality itself is beyond cognition. Our cognitive capacity knows and knows and knows, until it begins to approach a reality that it cannot know. And the reason it cannot know it is not because our cognitive capacity is not developed, or because there is something wrong with it, or even because there is an obscuration, but because the reality it is now encountering has nothing to do with knowing—it is beyond knowing. When the mind recognizes that to be the case, it basically bows down and bows out.

In some sense, the mind has been wanting to do that for a long time because it has been doing the difficult job of inquiry for so long and it needs to rest. It wants to go to sleep. It wants the world to run without it because it has been feeling that it has had to be in charge of everything.

So, we find out that one of the dimensions of our True Nature is that it is nonconceptual. We discover that we can be without the discernment, discrimination, and knowing of mind because presence and awareness are ultimately, primordially, nonconceptual. Reality exists without concepts, regardless of knowing or not knowing.

How do we make this discovery? As we learn more and more how to be where we are, and as we follow our personal thread, at some point the meaning of what is happening at any moment becomes nonconceptual. We are in the presence—we are presence—without the concept of presence; we are being here without thinking, "I am here." Now that is not to be confused with being distracted. You can be "not here," in the sense of being disconnected, and if someone points it out to you, you will recognize that you were somewhere far away. What I am talking about here is when you are quite aware of what is going on, but you are not self-reflecting in that place, not discriminating. And it is not that you don't have the capacity to discriminate; it is just that sometimes it is not necessary to do so. In the presence of that ground of nonconceptual being, reification simply does not happen; it actually can't happen because reification requires some kind of cognition. Any knowingness—even immediate knowingness, such as when we know the strength quality of presence by being it—has a conceptual component to it. But the strength essence can also appear without the cognitive capacity labeling it. The strength and the feeling of capacity and the inner heat are there, but your mind is not saying, "strength," "capacity," or "heat." Your mind is not saying anything. You just *are* strength. And, it is not lifeless or pale; it is alive, and it is glistening.

It is important to recognize that what we mean by "nonconceptual" here is not what most people, including philosophers, mean by this term. Usually, nonconceptual describes something that is not mental, but is rather immediate experience, like a feeling or sensation. So the scent of a flower will be seen as nonconceptual, the texture of the orange is nonconceptual. I refer to this level of experience as basic knowing, not as nonconceptual perception. In the way I am discussing things here, these experiences and perceptions are still conceptual, because there is knowing in them, and knowing always involves concepts, even when the concepts are those of gnosis—that is, spiritual immediate knowing.

What I am calling nonconceptual here is beyond immediate and nonrepresentational knowing. It is beyond basic knowing or gnosis. It is not a knowing at all, and there is no recognition of anything; it is total innocence of mind, perceiving but not recognizing what we are perceiving.

So, we see that we have the possibility of being where we are—to be in such nakedness, such purity, that we just are and that is that. And we don't even say "we" and "are"—everything just is as it is. The terminology used by those in the Eastern traditions is very good for indicating this, because it is just a pointing. You can ask, "What is it?"

and they will say, "It is *that*." Or "What is reality?" and the answer will be, "It is just thus."

No explanation is possible because there is nothing to explain, because there is nothing to discern—or, the discerning capacity does not function at that level. Awareness has gone deeper than discernment can go. It has reached the totally nonconceptual depth of True Nature, the noncognitive depth of reality. Thus we recognize that True Nature—the nature of everything—is fundamentally nonconceptual, beyond mind. And, the fact that awareness is beyond the mind means that we can be free of the mind.

FREEDOM FROM MIND

We cannot be free of the mind if there is only mind. If we have just the conceptual mind, there is no freedom. But the fact that awareness is beyond that conceptual mind, and we are that awareness, means that we are fundamentally free. It is just that we are almost always identified with the mind, so we remain in bondage to it.

If we can be without the mind even for a little while, many of the subtle obstacles and identifications, as well as the conceptualizations underlying our reifications, can be exposed. We can see the discrimination, the labeling, and how all of these activities are the natural activities of the mind—necessary for navigating our practical life but not necessary for us to be ourselves. To be who we are, we don't need these things. To be what we are—just to be, just to be alive—we don't need them.

But many people think that if mind is gone, there will be no experience. In fact, the opposite is true: awareness continues with more intensity, more clarity, more transparency; colors are more vivid and forms are much more distinct. That is because everything becomes much more itself, since all the veils, all the projections, all the concepts are gone. We perceive without anything intervening, so everything is naked as itself. To believe that when the mind is gone, we won't see anything, we must believe that everything exists only in our limited, discursive mind.

Hence, from the place that is beyond mind, we do not reify non-doing, because we don't conceptualize it. The awareness that is beyond mind cannot make any distinction between doing and non-doing because the distinction between doing and nondoing is conceptual; it involves knowing.

We see here the layer where conceptualization becomes the obstacle, the barrier. The reification of the concepts of doing and nondoing in this dimension of experience is not the barrier—the conceptualization itself, the knowing itself, is the obstacle. Actually, it is even more subtle than that. The knowing itself is not inherently an obstacle, but because it can easily become the ground for reification, it becomes the building block that the mind uses to reify.

But the mind doesn't have to be thrown out altogether. Our capacity to be in the nonconceptual makes it possible for us to use our mind and yet be free from the tendency to reify. Usually, we think that only the knowing mind exists. But both layers of awareness—the conceptual and nonconceptual, the cognitive and the perceptual—are always together. When we are able to discern and be in the nonconceptual, then the conceptual, discursive mind, may go away for a while. Sometimes when it returns, it no longer operates the same way as before; it can become an assistant to the perceptual awareness. And when it assists the perceptual awareness rather than replacing it, the discerning, discriminating awareness can operate through knowing without reification.

MOVING BEYOND KNOWING

Everything that we have discussed so far—the rejection, the comparative judgment, the attacks, the identifications, the attachments—is based, ultimately, on the reification of concepts. When we reify the body, we don't reify the body itself but our concept of the body; when we reify doing, we reify the concept of doing. It is always a mental picture that is reified; we cannot reify anything itself. We cannot do anything to reality; we can only do something about our conception of it.

So, because everything is based on reified concepts, it seems that we have arrived now at the most basic level of our difficulty—conceptualization itself, the knowing itself. Some spiritual traditions say that since the knowing is the beginning of all the problems, we should get rid of it; we need to throw away the knowingness. The problem with that is: we can throw it away for a while, but we cannot throw it away forever because it is part of us.

So how do we resolve this dilemma? We need to find out how to use the knowingness in a way that doesn't ensnare but liberates. The fact is that we need knowingness to get to enlightenment. Without knowingness, we would just become stupid saints. A cow is a kind of saint—she grazes peacefully, lies down when she has eaten enough, has no hatred for anything, doesn't want to kill anyone, is completely harmless. But a human being in that state would be called a stupid saint because the knowingness that brings in creativity and learning would be missing. Our human intelligence, our knowingness, our discerning capacity, is what opens many of our potentialities. But it is a double-edged sword; it can turn back on itself and cut us into pieces, disconnecting us from the primordial place of unity and innocence.

The more we learn to be in that place and not fight it, the freer we can be from the dangers of identification, reification, and the reactions that happen in the mind. How do we do that? If you remember, we cease fighting only by recognizing how we are fighting. And as we recognize where we are, without trying to change ourselves, we begin to have insight into our identification and reification. That process, at some point, reveals what underlies the reification—the inherent knowingness. And the inherent knowingness eventually reveals the pure, transparent, clear, empty light that is just the light of awareness and perception, which is fundamental to any experience.

So in the nonconceptual, pure light of awareness, there is no knowing, but there is no deficiency either. I don't become like a cow, and I am not a stupid saint. It is not that I don't know because there is something wrong with my brain, or because I am stupid or I lack information or I haven't inquired enough. The reason I don't know is that I am perceiving things from a place that is prior to knowing, that is more fundamental than knowing. When the knowing tries to go to that place, it just dissolves and becomes pure transparent light.

NOT KNOWING AND NO KNOWING

This place of not knowing is different than the not knowing we encounter in inquiry when we have a new experience or one we've had before but have not investigated. The latter is the kind of not knowing that we need to move through many times on our inner journey. We need to first recognize through our inquiry that we don't know something before we can begin to know it. So, for example, we cannot recognize our essential presence before realizing that we don't know what essential presence is. Because if we continue to believe that we know it, we will never find out what it actually is. So inquiry always requires letting ourselves experience that "I don't really know what this is . . . I don't know what is happening right now . . . I don't know who I am."

It is possible for us to be in that place and still be aware because the nonconceptual awareness is there. But that doesn't mean that we are aware of the nonconceptual dimension directly. The nonconceptual is supporting that process, but our conceptual, cognitive mind is still present—it just hasn't yet grasped something. It doesn't know, but it knows that it doesn't know. In contrast, in the nonconceptual you don't know and you don't know that you don't know. There is *no* knowing, where before there was *not* knowing.

So we could say that there are three different kinds of not knowing:

1. "I don't know, and I don't know that I don't know." This is pure ignorance and darkness, for I believe I know many things. The knowing mind is present.
2. "I don't know, and I know that I don't know." This is awakening to my condition.

3. "I don't know, and I don't know that I don't know." This is pure realization, light, no darkness, but the knowing mind is absent.

Zen masters have expressed these as: First there is a mountain, then there is no mountain, then there is a mountain.

On the journey, first we find out that we don't know. Then we begin to know. We come to know more and more until we pass through all the knowledge and beyond it. When we stay with our inquiry until everything—all the details—have been revealed, then we arrive at the source from which all the knowledge springs: the pure awareness, the pure light of our Being, where the mind is dissolved in wonder.

EXPLORATION SESSION

Knowing and Not Knowing

This exercise is an exploration of your basic orientation to knowing and not knowing. Give yourself at least fifteen minutes for this inquiry and more if you need it.

The first thing to consider is how knowing helps you to be yourself. In what ways do understanding and discrimination in your experience bring you more in contact with who you are?

Then consider the opposite. How does knowing get in the way of being yourself? This might include trying to know, believing you should know, holding on to past knowledge, describing your experience, using words—any way that knowing comes up for you as a hindrance.

Finally, take some time to consider not knowing. What are some of the ways you have experienced not knowing? How does not knowing affect you?

CHAPTER 17

To Be and Not to Be

IF WE LOOK AT ALL THE MENTAL operations we have been exploring that are helping us to better understand our experience, we are able to discern a particular inclination. Observing how our consciousness works, we can see that in every activity of the mind—whether it is conceptualizing, naming, labeling, reifying, identifying, reacting, rejecting, judging, grasping, or attaching—it is as if our mind wants to get away from something.

We have seen how when we reify and identify with something, we objectify it. We make it exist as an object, we make it concrete. This habit of mind reveals our movement toward objectifying and solidifying our experience. It would be natural for the mind to try to know reality, but it goes further than that; it always tries to pin it down, to establish it, to see reality as a concrete, stable thing. So we see that all our mental operations imply the same tendency—to try to solidify reality, objectify it, make it as concrete as a physical object is.

In general, what is most real for human beings is the physical. To us, a rock is something that actually exists; it is something to contend with. If everything else fails, we look for a big, solid rock—whatever we consider to be "the bedrock of reality." Why? Why don't we naturally move toward liquefying everything? Why don't we want to make everything gaseous, more like air? Why do we find the solid state preferable?

When you think about it, you realize that much of the universe and much of our own experience is not that solid. For example, our feelings are pretty fluid and hard to find. Our thoughts are even more so; they basically don't exist. They are more like ungraspable holograms. But those thoughts, those ungraspable holograms, always want to pin things down, make everything real and established and known in a concrete, storable way.

We can see how this habit becomes the tendency of the ego-self—or what we call the self—to preserve itself. The self is always looking for something concrete, something solid, stable, graspable, to support itself with, to depend on. That is because the self believes that if there is no bedrock, it is going to sink; if the bottom of reality is not solid, the self will get submerged and drown. So we believe that we have to locate some kind of island or rock of solidity to stand on to keep us from drowning.

LOOKING FOR SOMETHING SOLID

How does this relate to our practice of nondoing? From this perspective, the practice of nondoing basically becomes an undoing of this process of solidification. We just see through the various mental operations that conceptualize and grasp onto things in an attempt to make them solid and concrete. We make that process transparent, starting with observing the gross, surface level and moving to the deeper, more subtle subliminal processes.

Let's say I have an orange. I throw it to you, and you catch it. As soon as you conceptualize, "It is an orange that is being thrown to me now," you draw a boundary around it. To reify something means we make that boundary solid: it is this thing; it is an object called an orange. You think, "If I can catch an orange, if it can be thrown to me, it must really exist."

Imagine if somebody tossed an orange for you to catch, but instead it went through you. What would you think? "Did I die? I must be a ghost. All this time, I've been thinking I am alive, but that orange just went through me, so I must have been a ghost all along!" Your sense of self depends on solidity and boundaries to feel its existence.

Why do we have such a need to concretize? Because for us to orient ourselves, to feel a sense of reality, to operate, we feel that we need a foundation, a solid center, a base of operation. We believe that we need some place from which to spring into action. And we want our center of operation to be as stable, as solid, and as real as possible.

This tendency exists in every subtle operation of the mind. If I hate and reject something about myself, it is a way to separate myself from it. I tell myself, "I am not that—I am this other thing." Or I reify—I recognize this characteristic and start thinking of it and relating to it as though it really were an object.

We do this even with our True Nature. After a while, we think, "I have a True Nature . . . I have an essential nature . . . I have presence . . . and I remember its qualities." But in our memory, the qualities of True Nature are regarded as though they were tangible things. Presence becomes almost like an orange that we can throw and catch. So even when we discover our essential nature—when we recognize the light, or the presence, that exposes much of our illusory reality—we can end up reifying even that, making it into something solid. We do that to give ourselves a sense of reality.

It is interesting to watch how our consciousness gropes for something solid. At some point, it finds presence and says, "Well, at least I am not nothing. It is true that I have been imagining something to be real that is actually an image of the past. But now I have let it go and spaciousness has arisen. I recognize myself as I really am. I am truly full and present. What a relief!" We are relieved because for a while we were afraid that if we let go of the image, we would evaporate.

That is why some teachings have been reluctant to say that there is such a thing as True Nature. Because the moment I think of True

Nature, then there is me, there is True Nature, and I can sit on it. I can sit in it, I can stand in it, because it is a solid ground of reality. This idea gives us a feeling of security that we won't disappear. It gives us the recognition that we are not just a ghost, not just a hologram.

So we recognize here the subtle tendency in our consciousness to find a place that is somewhat opaque, somewhat solid, somewhat stable for us to stand on, so our mind can feel a sense of existence and presence. But at some point, that place can become a perch for the ego. Presence can, of course, be experienced as spaciousness, fluidity, radiance, or solidity. It can be all of these things, and it is never just one thing, because it is always changing and moving. But we need to understand what we usually end up doing with the notion of True Nature, of presence. We say that our practice is to be where we are, but we can reify that, too: "Be where I am? I've got it now! I know what to do—just find where I am and remain there."

The teaching of being where we are condones that; what's more, it encourages it. We finally feel good about being able to be where we are, and we are happy to have support to keep doing that. But when we don't understand how our mind works, we can't see that this is actually a way to continue being. The part of "to be where we are" that appeals to the ego is "to be," because that translates to us as, "I am going to continue to be." You might say to yourself, "I used to compare where I am to others, or to where I thought I should be, and now I am just where I am." But underneath that experience of being where you are is still the sense that "As long as I can continue being, I am okay." And what about the nonconceptual? "Great! I love the nonconceptual because I don't even have to think about it; I just continue being here." Because our mind is so intelligent and resourceful, that's how our thinking goes. Being where we are has then become a subtle strategy for the self-identity to find stability and solidity.

But if we are aware or attentive enough, if we are curious enough, we will catch what we are doing. Eventually, we will recognize this tendency to try to solidify everything and ask ourselves, "Why am I always doing that?" As soon as this inquiry arises, we will begin to see all the ways and the reasons why we try to solidify things. Maybe we are looking for approval or we want security. We think it is important to have land, possessions, family, children—anything that we can possess we make into something solid to rely on in order to continue being.

OUR ATTACHMENT TO POSITIONS

At some point in our inquiry, we recognize that we are carrying a certain attitude, one that we think can provide something we can turn into a base of operations. And attitudes easily move into being investments, positions. No matter what we do, if it is not completely spontaneous, natural, and without self-reflection, it will have an investment in it. So an attitude can become, for example, a position you take regarding a particular issue—a political issue, a philosophical issue, or any other kind of situation.

We all have positions, and we are very attached to them. Whatever happens, we have a position—for it, or against it, or "I've got my own position that is independent of everyone else's," or even, "Well, since I don't know all the facts, I really can't take sides; so I refuse to get involved." That is a position, too.

So what does having a position do for you? Why do we take positions? At first we may be focused on deciding what is correct or useful about specific issues: "I support capital punishment . . . I am against putting that halfway house in my neighborhood . . . I think abortion should be legal under this condition but not that one." But after a while, we find that any particular position we are taking has to do with how we see ourselves as much as how we're seeing a particular issue. We're not just taking up specific causes, we're fighting for the position that "I am a Republican" or "I am a Democrat" or "I am a Social Democrat." Our ideology has become important not only because it gives us a solid place to stand on an issue, but also because it provides us with an identity, a sense of self to operate from.

But a position doesn't have to be ideological or political. For example, if we say there is such a thing as a physical body, we assume that this is a fact, but actually it is a position. When it is an assumption from which we operate, it is a position. How about the statement, "I am a being of light"? That is a position. Now we've changed how we see ourselves: "I am not a physical body, I am a fluid being of light." But if you are really a fluid being of light, you don't need to defend that reality, you don't need to protect it. If somebody doesn't recognize what you are, it doesn't matter to you. So it's not something you have to take a position about.

But the moment we get concerned about a matter, the moment we believe that we have to defend our perceptions about it or our personal experience of it, we have taken a position. We have identified something around which we can collect ourselves.

Our tendency to look for something solid to perch on and anchor ourselves to amidst all our positions about things, can become a subtle, ongoing part of our normal everyday experience. But if support for our position is taken away, if we are challenged by someone else's position, or if they challenge or question ours, we can become feverish or obsessive about it.

Why is that? Because we are desperate to have a ground, a center to function from—which ultimately means having a self. We may never put it into words, but we feel, "I need something that is me, a place from which to function. I need a center that my thoughts can flow out of and touch the world, so the world can reflect something back to me." We want the world to be a mirror so we can look at it and find some reality in our reflection: "Yes, that is me! I am really here!" And we even do this with presence. Presence just is, but our consciousness can reflect it back in such a way that we can use it to say, "That's me. I exist."

FEAR OF THE BLACK HOLE

Why do we have this tendency to constantly look for validation of our self-existence? What is behind all these efforts to constellate around anything we think we can rely on to keep confirming that we *are*? If we continue with our inquiry into this, at some point we may feel fear, perhaps even terror, and that fear shows us that we are running away from something. We feel that something we don't understand is running after us, and we are scared to death. It is as if we are always trying to climb up out of a deep, dark pit. We are trying to find something, anything, to grab on to or get a foothold on, so that we don't slide all the way down to the bottom. If we explore those feelings, we discover that what we are trying to climb out of is a black hole. We are terrified that the black hole will suck us in.

We somehow can sense that nobody ever escapes the black hole! So we hope that we will be able to stay outside the event horizon beyond the influence of the black hole. Remember, the event horizon is the point inside of which objects, experiences, and even light cannot escape because they get sucked in by the overwhelming gravity of the black hole.

But we can never find our security in trying to climb out; it's not even possible to climb out, because this black hole is not located in space. It is everywhere. And it turns out that our effort to run away or to climb out or to escape is an attempt to continue being, as we understand it. When we investigate the omnipresent nature of presence, we understand this to mean that we are not doing anything, but our mind can still interpret that nondoing as an "activity" of being there, as the expression of having some kind of concrete existence.

But that is not the true meaning of True Nature, of presence. When we explore what presence feels like, when we experience its luminosity, we recognize that, though it can feel substantial, it has no substance; it is not solid at all. Even though, when we first encounter it, we know that presence is what truly exists, our mind mistakenly conceives of its existence in the same way that we think a rock exists. But in doing that, we reify it, we concretize it, and miss its very nature. So we take presence to be existence, but the existence of presence is not like the existence of the body, for example, because it is not an object. Even though we say that presence is our being, that it is the authentic ontological ground of our consciousness, neither being nor existence are what we are referring to when we speak of the existence of a rock or a chair. We need to be very subtle in our understanding of what "presence is being" means. We need to recognize the pitfall of the tendency to objectify.

This tendency to objectify is always an attempt to get away from this truth, from this reality that I am referring to as the black hole. And we are always trying to get away from it because it is always here; we cannot escape it. And somehow we are aware of that inescapability, we intuit it. We are continuously trying to create solidity because if we let ourselves completely relax, we will find out that the nature of presence itself is completely, absolutely nothing—it is more nothing than the nothing of empty space. It is nonbeing itself. So even though presence feels like being, when you recognize it, it is nonconceptual and therefore it is not—cannot be—the opposite of nonbeing. The notion of an opposite does not exist in the nonconceptual, and neither do being and nonbeing, because they are conceptual.

So, first we recognize that being is really fundamentally a nonbeing, nothing, absence. Presence turns out to be the other side of what can only be described as a spacious absence. The ground of the ground, the ground of presence itself, of the luminosity itself, is nonexistence. You feel it . . . it exists. But what is the feeling of existence in it? What makes it exist? What is the ground of the existence of presence? The recognition of the fact that it does not exist, that it is absolutely nothing. Complete transparency, no opaqueness, no thickness, no objects, no solidity, no substance, no mass, no atoms, no time, no space . . . nothing.

But we get accustomed to believing in and living according to our ideas of what we think our existence is—an objective existence such as that of a rock. Thus, recognizing the actual underlying nature of our existence—the nonbeingness of it—requires such a subtle understanding that we tend not to see it.

THERE IS NO GROUND

The truth of our existence reveals itself only when we start to wonder why we are always moving toward solidity. If we inquire into this, we can follow the thread of why we keep doing it, as if something were pushing us toward reifying, objectifying, making things concrete. Why don't we just relax and let things be whatever they are? Because if we really did that, we would discover that the whole universe is just an event horizon. We would sense the infinite nothingness "within" all of reality. All of our experience, everything that manifests, is existing just on the edge of a huge black void of absence. It is all a glimmering surface of an infinite black hole, meaning that all of existence is a hologram, an insubstantial hologram.

What would happen if you didn't try to squeeze yourself into something solid and just let yourself relax? Just by relaxing, you would realize that things start to feel lighter. If you continue, everything becomes so light, so free, so transparent, that it feels as though you could put your hand through it. You can see through everything—and behind everything there is nothing, absolutely nothing. That is why you cannot see anything—because there is nothing. You look and it is pitch dark, like the universe before the Big Bang—no stars, no light, nothing there. But that nothingness is really the back of everything we see; everything you see is just the front. In fact, it doesn't really have a back at all.

So all our attempts at conceptualization, reification, identification, rejection, are ways of trying to make the hologram solid because we think that is what reality is, and we think that is how we can exist. We are not yet comfortable being an emptiness. We are not comfortable living with nothingness. Our soul, our consciousness, still doesn't know how to be settled without being settled on top of something. It doesn't know how to be on nothing or how to just float. We always have to sit someplace. We haven't recognized that if we feel our nature completely, we don't need to sit anywhere, and we don't need a ground of any kind.

And that is how it is anyway—there is no ground. It is not as though somebody is going to take reality away from us; nobody is going to take anything from us. All that will happen is that we will see through our belief, our position, that there is being and nonbeing. We will see through the illusion that there is existence and nonexistence. We will see through our attachment to the idea that we exist now but that nonexistence means we are going to disappear, that our existence is going to terminate.

But these are all concepts, conceptualizations, and reality is nothing like that. Reality is this: We are here and not here at the same time, absolutely. We don't exist and we continue to exist. This doesn't make sense to our mind because of our conceptual positions. We carry a deep conviction that if we don't exist, we cannot eat, we cannot talk, we cannot do anything. Don't you believe that if you don't exist, then it's all over for you, that you can't live? But reality is not like that. Reality is: You don't exist and you keep on living. You die and are born again even though you don't exist.

So how are we going to get comfortable with this? First of all, we cannot get it with our minds; let us start with knowing that. If we try to wrap our mind around it, it will become a reification. It has to be something that stings you, just like a bee. When it happens, you don't know what hit you; you just jump. Then you have the recognition, the thought, "Oh, it's a sting . . . it's a bee." Reality is a bee sting before the concept of a bee sting.

So, when we recognize this, then all we do is practice being where we are—but now we remember that being where we are doesn't mean what we used to think it did. It doesn't mean that it is "me" who is going to be there; that is just a way of talking, of referring to something.

So I am taking us one step further here toward understanding what is happening—by looking at our language, by looking at our practice, and by considering the practitioner as well. Remember that we also need to investigate what "we" means and what "are" means, when we talk about being where we are. So when we sit and meditate, we don't come with the idea that there is somebody who is going to sit. We just come to sit. Because being there means not doing anything to reality. We just leave everything alone.

Now if we don't do anything to reality, and we don't reify not doing, what will we find? Absolutely nothing. And finding absolutely nothing, we will be completely happy. We will discover that we cannot possess nothing, and neither can anybody else.

I am not saying that you should believe me about this. I don't think you can. This is something to be discovered for yourself. I am just giving you a hint. What is left is for you to find out for yourself.

EXPLORATION SESSION

Exploring Fluidity and Solidity in Your Experience

This is an opportunity to explore the potential for fluidity in your experience. Begin by spending several minutes being present with and observing your immediate experience, allowing whatever arises in your moment-to-moment awareness.

Next, take some time to consider the following questions: Did you notice any tendency to solidify what you became aware of? Did you find yourself labeling, associating with, engaging in inner dialogue about, preferring, judging? What other forms did solidification take in you? Is it possible for you not to break your experience into objects or make yourself into an object? Feel free to return to an awareness of your immediate experience as you explore these questions.

The more you refrain from solidifying or objectifying, the more open your experience will become. It will be less defined, less determined by your mind, and more unknown. What stops you from allowing your experience to be completely open at each moment? Is fear involved in limiting the openness? Keep noticing how you feel as you engage in this inquiry.

CHAPTER 18

The Preciousness
of Each Moment

Trueue Nature is the teacher, the Supreme Teacher. It is always teaching about its truth. All beings are its students, and it teaches every moment, for the experience of each moment is its teaching. True Nature is always manifesting its truth in one form or another. It cannot help but do that. It is its nature to reveal its essence, its truth. We only need to see it, recognize it. We see this manifestation of True Nature as our experience, but the experiences we have are just the momentary forms of how True Nature is continuously presenting its truth.

So each moment of our life is the teaching. And we can see what the teaching is if we allow ourselves to be where we are. When we are asking, "What is the meaning of my life?" we can see what it is if we allow ourselves to be where we are. Then we are seeing what True Nature is manifesting at every moment. And if we can truly and fully be where we are, then we realize that no moment is better than any other moment. Each moment is—all moments are—the expression of True Nature. There is nobody else, nothing else, that is manifesting anything.

Thus, each moment of our life is the teaching. And each moment has its own value because each moment is really the way that True Nature is manifesting itself, the way it is appearing, the form it is taking. We have seen that when we recognize the truth of our experience, the meaning appears and we can recognize that meaning. When we see the truth and abide in it, we recognize its value. So we look for meaning in our life—what the value of life is—but the fact is that it is not somewhere waiting to be discovered; it is always here. We just need to recognize that it is here.

At the beginning of our journey, when we are not able to be ourselves, value appears more in terms of what our mind thinks is valuable. But when we are real, when we are genuine, sincere, we recognize that true value is actually the same as recognizing the truth of the moment. Then we experience a kind of value that is not mental, that is heartfelt, that makes our heart feel satisfied.

As we progress on the journey, we recognize that the value of the experience is where we are, the presence of where we are. True Nature manifests its value directly by revealing its presence, not by camouflaging it in one form or another. Eventually, we reach the advanced stages of the journey where it is revealed that everything is itself and its nature—and hence inherently valuable, inherently beautiful, inherently precious. At that point, we realize that all manifestations, whether we can recognize them specifically or not, *are* that inherent value and preciousness of reality.

At the first stage, our experiences are of the same kind that we encounter in the advanced stages, but we just don't recognize them for what they are. We can only begin to recognize value when we discern truth, when we see meaning. When we see the meaning of our experience, a heart satisfaction, a sense of valuing what it is, naturally arises. Even in difficult or painful experiences, when we are able to understand and learn from them, we recognize value that we couldn't have imagined at an earlier stage. This value is not the value of gaining more money or recognition or even love; it's closer to our heart than that, more heartfelt.

We are always looking for that sense of value to make our experience worthwhile, so that we can feel that we are worthy, but we often suffer the absence or the limitation of worthwhile-ness, of the sense of value, because we do not see ourselves clearly. We don't recognize who and what we are and we don't know how to be where we are. We are distant from where we are, fighting where we are. Whatever the value is that we want—whether it is fame or love or success or enlightenment or a specific experience—we think that it is something we have to accomplish. We believe we have to go someplace to get it, when it is right here, right in this very moment, if we just relax and be in it.

If we relax in this moment and be completely in it, we begin to recognize that *this* moment is reality, that *each* moment is reality, and this reality is the most valuable thing, the most precious thing, because it is the way that True Nature is manifesting. True Nature isn't waiting for us to succeed in our practice for it to be here. It is already here. Remember, it is beyond time.

VALUE WITHOUT CAUSE

This book opened with a discussion of the appreciation for being real. We saw how natural it is that when the heart, the feeling center of the human soul, is touched by realness, when it feels reality, it responds with love, with appreciation, with liking and enjoyment. Now we can see that it also responds by recognizing that realness has value that is beyond the mind; it has an intrinsic worth that cannot be measured in worldly things.

This value is beyond words and impacts us at a place that is beyond our worldly life. That is why, after a life of strife and pain and difficulty, many people finally have a glimpse of True Nature and find that one moment of recognition is worth all the suffering that went before. For some reason, this knowing fills our heart with a fullness, a sweetness, a sense of recognition of the inherent value of existence.

So you see, the value of existence at each moment is not the result of something else; it is its own nature, its own reality. It is not a matter of cause and effect. We do not value something because of something else. At the beginning stages of our work, we might be unclear or a little deluded and think that the reason we value reality is because it gives us a great experience or it makes us happy or it opens up some new capacities or it gives us some other benefit. It is true that it does all that. But the more clearly we recognize what is manifesting in the moment—what the meaning of the moment is, what teaching is manifesting through any particular form—the more we recognize that the very existence, the factness, the pure, self-existing value of each moment, is not related to a reason. Its value does not come from doing this or that; its value is inherent.

When we recognize this inherent value of reality, when we experience it ourselves, our heart cannot help but be suffused with a sense of appreciation. And it's not that we value it because we think it is great. The value is not something that I give to or impose on reality; the value is reality itself—or reality is the value.

It is not that it's valuable *because* it is transparent and luminous and free and light; its own intrinsic nature makes experience and life supremely worthwhile. It makes every moment seem full of treasures, treasures that the mind cannot fathom. And those treasures are not someplace in the future but in the moment. Knowing this is simply a matter of recognition. It is a matter of being able to see clearly.

THE SOURCE OF ALL VALUE

We have said that the things that appear in our experience at the early stages of the journey are the same as in the later stages when reality reveals itself directly. In those beginning stages, veils are in the way, keeping us from seeing things directly, preventing us from seeing them completely and accurately. Instead we see our experience through all our reifications. But each form that appears at any stage of the journey is True Nature manifesting something to us in order to reveal itself—even veils and obscurations, barriers and obstacles. Every experience is here to teach us.

So the issue is: How good a student of experience are we at each moment? And what does it mean to be a good student? To practice, to learn, means to perceive the teaching that is coming through each moment of our life—not just during a meditation retreat or while reading this book or doing the practice exercises or pursuing our inquiry, but in each moment of our life. There needs to be no differentiation or separation of these activities from the rest of our life.

A good student is one who recognizes that in every moment, everything that happens—whether we think it is bad or good, painful or pleasurable—is nothing but True Nature teaching, manifesting its truth. The more we recognize this, the more our soul becomes suffused with the juices, the nectars, of fulfillment and satisfaction. The more real it becomes to us, the more our heart becomes full and pregnant with the natural fruition of recognizing the truth. We begin to recognize that we are all children of the moment, which means we are all children of True Nature.

So when we are learning the practice of being where we are, we recognize at some point that we won't be able to pay attention to where we are if we don't value the moment. If we don't recognize that each moment has nutrition, has truth that helps us grow, we won't be able to let ourselves be where we are.

At the beginning of our practice, we're seeking the insights, the recognitions, the significant details of particular experiences as if these were what brings value. As we go on, we recognize that all these are coming from the presence of True Nature. Presence is actually what has value, what is value. We discover that the presence of True Nature is self-existing worth, self-existing value. It is its own value, and the source of all value.

As we come to recognize that intrinsic value, we can see that the teaching is appearing through everything—and we not only appreciate the moment, we will make sure never to ignore it or neglect it. We will seize the moment and learn not to waste it, not to distract ourselves. And I don't mean that we will spend twenty hours a day sitting in meditation or go live in a monastery. I mean that we will be where we are and appreciate being real, recognizing what is really happening and seeing as much truth as possible in the moment.

When we don't see where we are, we can be in the moment, but we are not seeing it clearly; we are running away from it, we are distracted, we are abandoning ourselves. When we are real, we let ourselves be where we are. And when we recognize where we are—for where we are is the moment as it is appearing clearly—we are allowing ourselves to be suffused by the teaching. And the more we recognize the value of the moment, the more our heart will open, revealing its depth, its fullness, its richness.

At first, our mind tries to explain why we love recognizing the truth, why we value reality and True Nature, why we think it is wonderful, beautiful, supportive, and something that liberates us. But all these are just conceptual stories we tell ourselves. The fact is that True Nature's value is inherent, beyond the mind, and we are just feeling it. And there is no reason for it. It is, and that is the way it is.

So, as you see, the teaching has that value because it arises from True Nature; it is the message of True Nature. And our learning is not restricted to what comes through a particular logos—although specific, defined channels of teaching do exist and can be helpful. The real teaching of True Nature is every moment.

THE DIFFICULTY OF
EXPERIENCING VALUE

I know that it is difficult for us sometimes to let ourselves experience this inherent value in the moment. To value the moment means that it is okay to value ourselves, to recognize ourselves as worth it, as deserving this richness—and we have issues, questions, and beliefs about valuing ourselves. Many of us have painful or difficult histories. Certain experiences, beliefs, and projections make us feel that we are not worth it, we are not good enough, or that we have to do one thing or another to receive or assign to ourselves any value or esteem. That leads to the belief that we have to try, we have to make an effort, we have to suffer a lot and tread a long path before we can arrive at what is valuable, at what the true value and meaning of life is.

But all these are just issues, obscurations, that have nothing to do with the truth. Value is True Nature and True Nature is what we are. Valuing the moment is valuing ourselves, is valuing our nature, is valuing everybody and everything.

To recognize inherent value, to experience it directly, is the same thing as being in the immediacy of the moment. And this is what allows our True Nature to manifest itself in a way that fulfills the heart, that fulfills life. We feel a sense of an inherent value. We understand that we don't have to accomplish a thing in our life for our life to be worthwhile. Whether or not we have success, invent something, accomplish some difficult feat, create a great piece of art, write a bestseller, or become famous is secondary. None of those things is necessary for us to recognize our sense of value because value is not something that is accomplished; it is already here.

This experience or recognition of a sense of worth, of a sweet fullness and deep fulfillment, doesn't make sense to the mind. We grew up learning that our sense of esteem, our sense of value, is a result of a cause. We were taught that we have to be "good" or do things in a certain way or learn or accomplish whatever someone else thinks is valuable; otherwise life has no worth.

So although value is an inherent experience in our heart of the recognition of our nature, there are obstacles that keep us from being in touch with it. Some of those come from the injunctions of our childhood, some of them result from positions we have taken or judgments we have made. Regardless of the cause, we end up missing whatever value, whatever nutrition, whatever beauty there is in the moment. And, that is really sad—not bad, just sad. It is sad that we cannot recognize the value inherent in the moment and therefore don't allow ourselves the enjoyment that reality makes possible each moment.

But when we really recognize ourselves and let ourselves be in the moment, we come into an amazing freedom that brings in a sense of a natural appreciation of just what is. Then we can accomplish and do all kinds of things, not to achieve value, only to express it.

It is the other way around from what we thought, you see? We have the treasures in us, and every moment is a matter of expressing them. And expressing them is a matter of participating with True Nature in revealing itself. We let ourselves be servants, conduits for True Nature to reveal its teaching. So, the more we accept where we are and let ourselves be where we are and the less we fight the moment and recognize it for what it is, then the more effective conduits we are for True Nature to teach us, and teach through us, directly.

So the teaching is happening in every way that experience appears. As you may have noticed, when you are inquiring, you discover at some point the meaning of what you are experiencing. Everything has meaning, and meaning is always there. Nothing is haphazard. Everything has a precise order. That is why I tend to agree with Einstein that reality is not probability, that God doesn't throw dice. Everything has a precise order, every single little thing has a meaning in the order of things—and all of it is revealing the truth of reality.

INQUIRY AS A REVELATION
OF IMPLICIT VALUE

What inquiry does is show us this meaning. We see that everything is interconnected—one fabric of revelation. With that understanding, we are able to recognize what is being revealed. When we get the revelation, we can't help but feel satisfied and capable of valuing our experience regardless of how painful or difficult it may have been.

We begin our journey of inquiry feeling that we value our experience because we have learned from it; we say that we have grown from it. That is true, but it's just a way of explaining it. All that our learning means is that we are getting closer to the self-existing value. When we recognize the self-existing value, which is True Nature itself, we recognize that the fact that we have learned, that we have grown, is a side effect, a reflection of the true value and meaning of existence. Yes, the meaning first appears as relative, but at some point we recognize that the meaning is *us*—all of us.

So it doesn't matter what is happening in the moment. No moment is better than any other moment. No one's experience is better than another person's experience. Your experience in the moment is the way True Nature is teaching. It is not accurate to say, "That guy is at a more advanced place than I am, so I should be like him." You are comparing yourself and making a judgment that your experience is not as valuable—and so the sense of your own value is lost. No, your experience is the right teaching at that moment for you, and for the rest of reality, too. Your experience is just as valuable, just as necessary, as the experience of somebody supposedly more advanced on the path or having more sublime experiences.

The more we learn that each moment has its own intrinsic value, the easier it is for us to let ourselves just be in each moment, however it is manifesting. Then we recognize that where we are is where we are supposed to be. Are you sad? Bursting with excitement? Feeling sexual? Having an attack of jealousy? Tired and cranky? Feeling hopeless, inadequate, or afraid? Or are you sitting on top of the world? Well, then, that is what reality is manifesting. Who are we to judge that we shouldn't be that way? Who are we to say that we should be like some other person?

We may find it useful to recognize where we are in relationship to the whole picture, but that doesn't change the fact that each place has its own value. Something is being revealed in this moment that isn't going to be revealed in any other place or time or through any other person, and it is just as necessary as what is happening to someone else or what will be happening to you a minute, a month, or many years from now.

Value is truly nothing other than our heart's intimate contact with the immediacy of the moment—with each moment, with where we are precisely. In that contact, in that being with and knowing reality as it is, we recognize the unquestionable rightness and preciousness of where we are and what we are.

Nothing touches us more deeply than the implicit value of our own beingness. It is value beyond mind, beyond concepts, beyond ideals and hopes and dreams. This preciousness of simply being here now with awareness and understanding fills our heart with contentment and satisfaction. We realize that where we are, which is what we are, is also the most real and precious nature of life itself.

EXPLORATION SESSION

Discovering How You Value Present Experience

This exercise is an opportunity to explore the way value plays a part in your practice of being where you are.

First, look at why you do not value the moment. What stops you from feeling the preciousness of each moment in your experience and instead makes you prefer some moments, certain experiences, and particular situations and times over others? Becoming more aware of this will help you to see more about how you value your time, your experiences, and yourself in your life.

Second, explore the various ways in which you experience the value in being where you are. How is it worthwhile for you to be present with yourself, to not go away, to feel what is here, to be in the moment? You may not value it all the time, but by now you have certainly touched on the preciousness of being here, being present, being more real. This is a time to articulate that sense of preciousness.

Afterword

WHEN WE CONSIDER OUR life, it is generally from the vantage point of where we are now: we make assessments about where we have come from, what we have accomplished, and where we are going. How far have we progressed? Have we done enough to feel satisfied? What goals still remain to be pursued?

We identify and evaluate the status of our life in relation to our physical environment, our relationship circumstances, our financial status, our goal achievement, and our physical health, among other things. All of these means of establishing where we are in our life locate us in the physical, external world by relating us to elements of our life that we believe control our well-being. Even when we locate ourselves by observing our emotional condition or our mental activity, these elements are usually experienced as reactions to what is going on in our external life.

In other words, we assume that the most significant determinants of where we are in our life are the external factors; it is these that become the measuring stick of our development, our progress, and even our happiness in life. But even more significant is the fact that they become central to how we define who we are.

This book has offered a different orientation to the question of where you are in life—specifically, where you are in the moment. This approach is a spiritual exploration because it focuses on the location of your consciousness rather than your body, your beliefs, your pocketbook, or your significant others. The goal of these teachings has not been to help you evaluate how well you have succeeded or help you decide where to go next. It has been to support you in discovering where you are, so you can simply *be* where you are. Because it is by being where you are in an easy, relaxed way that you can truly discover who and what you are.

This process of locating yourself is a profoundly personal one, a subtle and sensitive unfolding of inner awareness that does not use obvious external signposts to tell you where you are at any given time. It requires discipline and patience, gentleness and attunement, because the only one who can know where your consciousness is is you. To truly be where you are requires a capacity for listening, a willingness to be open, and a curiosity about your own experience that most likely few people have ever shown toward you.

What this calls for is the development of your ability to truly witness yourself, to be a pure and undistorted mirror for where and how you are appearing in the moment. Ultimately, this means seeing yourself without the aid of anyone else's perspective, anyone else's experience, or anyone else's beliefs and judgments. It means not seeing yourself from the outside or locating yourself by where you are relative to external criteria. It is by seeing yourself from inside, from the center of your own experience, that you can discover your own truth, the untouched True Nature of what you are.

This understanding is the heart of *The Unfolding Now* and has shaped its primary function: to act as a transitional mirror. The fact is that when we begin the inner journey, the capacity of our awareness to recognize itself is limited, so we need outside mirrors for a while. We do not even know our True Nature exists, much less how to recognize it, or that it is what we truly are. Our awareness is not developed enough to be able to stand on its own and to recognize its nature. So it needs mirroring to see past its own limitations. That is one reason why people join spiritual schools or go on retreats.

The real mirror—which is the self-awareness you are cultivating in learning to mirror yourself—is to see yourself without judgment, without comparison, without self-hatred, without reification, and without conceptualization, but with compassion and courage and kindness and love and presence and awareness and intelligence. The teachings in this book have been offered as support for the process of becoming your own mirror in these different ways. They can help you develop the confidence that you can learn to sit and meditate, to inquire, to recognize yourself where you are, to see your own personal thread and be able to remain with it so that it unfolds and reveals the truth of what you truly are—your True Nature.

This is a practice that requires a sustained meditative, focused exploration apart from the activities of daily life. It takes quiet times of attention and reflection to develop the subtle attunement in our soul to our inner whereabouts. Only after continued regular practice with concentrated attention to our ongoing experience can our contact with presence withstand the constant distractions of our own busyness.

However, if we follow the thread of being aware and present as our practice of learning to be where we are, we might be able to increase the time or the space where we can be ourselves in an open way, extending it beyond the quiet, secluded moments. The more we remember to practice awareness of ourselves, and the stronger the awareness in our presence, the more we are able to stay open and attuned to what is arising in our consciousness even as we live our lives.

Of course, it also means that we need to consider the life we live and how we are living it. What takes us away from just being where we are? What do we value instead of valuing the truth of the moment? Where does our attention go? How much of our resources of time and energy are actually needed for taking care of the necessities of daily life? What do we lose by turning away from where we are now? Exploring these questions becomes a process of integrating presence into the rest of our life.

So, our practice is a process of settling deeper into the moment and learning more about what takes us away from it. The mirror of our awareness gradually becomes less obscured and more luminous as it reveals to us the preciousness of what we truly are.

The capacity of this teaching to transform your own life can extend out to affect your environment, changing the way that you relate to other people and the world at large. As you come to appreciate and value True Nature and know it for the mysterious and limitless source of life that it is, it impacts and transforms your own manifestation as a person. True Nature can express itself through you more directly, touching others and opening up the richness and possibility of what it means to be human. That is one way that the flame is passed on, that the light is spread. In my experience, this is the most effective way to support a deeper change in the condition of consciousness in our world.

Our aim here is to be the realness that we love, to be as human as possible and to take that out into our life. The more of us who actually learn about reality and our own True Nature, the more others will recognize the preciousness and value of just being. Because, in fact, we are not separate, and True Nature is the nature of everyone. Each individual can come to value True Nature not just in themselves, but in everybody and everything. And when this appreciation is embraced and integrated, it will create expanding ripples moving out from each person.

And all of this can happen as you learn to simply be yourself in an easy, gentle way—at each moment, wherever you are.

Appendix

FOR THOSE FAMILIAR WITH the Diamond Approach through involvement in the Ridhwan School or through reading other books of A. H. Almaas, it may be of interest to place the teaching of this book in the larger context of this spiritual path.

The Unfolding Now is an experiential teaching based on the wisdom of one of the Diamond Dimensions, also known as the Diamond Vehicles. These are described on page 234 in *The Inner Journey Home*. This particular Diamond Dimension is the Point Diamond dimension of Essence. It brings a wisdom that is based on the realization of the Essential Identity, also known as the Point. (See *The Point of Existence* for a detailed discussion of this manifestation of Being and its realization.)

Each Diamond Dimension includes all of the essential aspects—the discriminated qualities of our True Nature—within it. This means that each individual aspect contributes its particular wisdom to the fundamental understanding provided by that particular Dimension or Vehicle. The Point Diamond dimension supports the soul's development through the knowledge that the more one allows oneself to be exactly where one is without interference or manipulation, the more the True Nature of the soul reveals itself. And so each aspect of Essence offers a particular wisdom about the truth of being where one is and the way this truth reveals the depth of who and what one is. Chapter 10 in *Spacecruiser Inquiry: True Guidance for the Inner Journey* gives more description of the Point Diamond Dimension.

What follows is a list of the eighteen chapters of this book and the specific aspect that imparts the teaching of that chapter. Most aspects have both a conceptual name and an experiential name, which can be used interchangeably. Chapter 6 includes two aspects. Chapters 11, 16, and 17 are teachings from the boundless dimensions rather than from the essential aspects.

The effectiveness of the teaching is in no way based on knowing this information, but the knowledge may support a greater understanding of the intelligence of Being and how it is experienced in the Diamond Approach.

CHAPTER	ASPECT
1	PERSONAL LOVE / *Pink*
2	OBJECTIVITY / *Clear*
3	WILL / *Silver*
4	SPACE
5	VULNERABILITY / *Water*
6	COMPASSION / *Green* AND STRENGTH / *Red*
7	TRUTH / *Gold*
8	ACCEPTANCE / *Aquamarine*
9	POWER / *Black*
10	KNOWING / *Blue*
11	SUPREME
12	NONDUAL PRESENCE / *Rigpa*
13	INTELLIGENCE / *Brilliancy*
14	CHANGE / *Mercury*
15	ESSENTIAL IDENTITY / *Point*
16	NONCONCEPTUAL
17	ABSOLUTE
18	VALUE / *Amber*

The Diamond Body Series

THIS SERIES OF BOOKS is an attempt to outline the methodology of the Diamond Approach, a contemporary spiritual teaching with its own direct understanding and view of reality. The Diamond Body series refers to the practice and embodiment of the Diamond Approach, as a complement to the Diamond Heart series, which pertains to the direct experience of True Nature on this path, and the Diamond Mind series, which relates to the objective knowledge and conceptual understanding of this teaching.

The series range from direct discussion of methodology, to the illustration of various applications within different contexts, to the integration of some of the classical methods of spiritual work into this teaching. Some of the volumes in this series illustrate the methodology through actual work on elements of the body of knowledge that is unique to the Diamond Approach teaching, such as the aspects of spiritual essence, the dimensions of reality, and the facets of mind.

To appreciate the place and function of the methodology in any approach to spiritual work, we need to understand how the methodology relates to the view of reality on which it is based and to the teaching that arises from that view. This understanding will help clarify the role of this series of books in the revelation of the Diamond Approach.

Throughout history, human beings have felt the need for intentional, focused work and guidance, to be able to advance beyond the average human development known in most societies. Much of our human potential lies in realms not accessible or even visible to normal consciousness. This is specifically the case for humanity's spiritual potential, which is the ground of human consciousness and the source of true and lasting fulfillment, peace, and liberation.

This situation has led to the rise and development of many teaching schools throughout the ages, inner-work schools that specialize in the development of the total human being—particularly the actualization of the depth of human potential. Such a spiritual school is usually built on a teaching that emerges from a specific logos—a direct understanding of reality and the situation of human beings within that reality. Through the teaching, the logos reveals a path toward the actualization of our human potential. The methodology of the path also reflects the wisdom arising from this direct understanding. It is not just a haphazard collection of techniques aimed at helping students to arrive at certain inner states. The methodology will be successful in unfolding the path when it is a faithful expression of the particular logos of that teaching. You could say that practicing the methodology of a teaching is the specific key needed to open the door of this teaching's logos of experience and wisdom.

This understanding of the relationship between logos, teaching, method, and reality has another important implication. As a methodology is practiced within the logos of a particular teaching, objective reality will reveal itself in forms relevant for the journey of self-realization undertaken through that teaching. In other words, a profound and fundamental manifestation of reality characteristic of one teaching may never arise for followers of a different teaching, because each teaching orients to reality through a different logos. One way of understanding this is that because each teaching traverses different terrain in its unfolding journey, the same underlying reality will be revealed in different forms along the way.

Consider, for example, that the Inuit people of the Arctic Circle recognize more than twenty forms of snow and ice. These are true forms of physical reality never recognized by someone living in temperate latitudes, because the climate and the demands of the environment are different. In a similar way, followers of a spiritual teaching will encounter distinct experiences of objective reality that are appropriate to the journey of the soul addressed by that teaching.

This awareness is especially important in understanding descriptions of essential reality in the books that come out of the Diamond Approach. The methodology of the Diamond Approach prepares the soul to experience, perceive, and appreciate that Being appears not only as needed at any given point in the soul's journey, but also in specific forms—which we call essential aspects—that arise in response to the constantly changing needs of the individual soul. However, though these states and qualities are referred to as universal and fundamental to all human souls and to reality itself, this does not mean that people engaged in deep spiritual work based on another logos will encounter reality in the form of essential aspects. Other teachings align the soul for traversing other paths of realization, and so essential reality may appear differently.

The central thread of wisdom informing the methodology of the Diamond Approach is that our normal human consciousness does not possess the knowledge or skill necessary for traversing the inner path of realization. However, the intelligence of our underlying spiritual ground tends to spontaneously guide our consciousness and experience toward liberation. This spiritual ground, which is the ultimate nature of reality, is unconditionally loving and compassionate in revealing its treasures of wisdom to whoever is willing to open to it. We simply need to recognize the truth about our present experience and learn the attitudes and skills that will invite the True Nature of reality to reveal itself. Toward that end, this methodology brings together classical spiritual techniques and new practices that can help us be open and vulnerable to our True Nature.

The task of communicating the teaching and logos for this method is the central function of the Ridhwan School, its teachers, and all the literature of the Diamond Approach. Like any genuine spiritual teaching, the degree to which this logos reveals itself depends on how faithfully the method is applied. And the skill in applying the methodology develops over time as the experience and understanding of the teaching matures.

However, since this method arises from a true logos of reality and therefore is inherent to objective reality, it is available for anyone to learn regardless of whether they are in contact with the Ridhwan School—if they are able to recognize the truth of this view for themselves. This means that it is possible to connect to this logos and practice its particular method by seriously studying the teaching on one's own. To do so, however, requires an unusual degree of sincerity, devotion, and intelligence. Such is the limitation of the printed word, in contrast to the direct transmission that can occur when one is in contact with an exemplar of the teaching. Hence, we can only hope for limited benefits when the method is practiced apart from the active guidance of the teaching and the teacher.

Still, we believe there is value in providing some understanding of the methodology of the Diamond Approach. This is not only for the benefit of the students directly engaged in this work, but also for readers who would like to learn and practice some of the elements of the method on their own. In addition, we hope this series will be useful in appreciating the contribution of this approach to an overall understanding of reality, human nature, and what it means to actualize humanity's full potential.

Because the heart of this methodology is a disciplined invitation to reality to reveal its secrets, the Diamond Body series offers the unique benefit of supporting both the pursuit of the inner path of realization and the exploration of the deeper principles of investigation and study that are relevant in any research discipline. Using elements of the Diamond Approach methodology can lead not only to a quickening and an openness to aspects of our inner potential, but also to the development of skills that can be useful for study in other fields within the sciences and humanities.

This is the universal message of the Diamond Approach: When we learn how to invite our True Nature to reveal itself, it will guide us toward realizing our spiritual ground and, at the same time, actualize our potential in all walks of life.

About the Diamond Approach

The Diamond Approach is taught by Ridhwan teachers, ordained by the Ridhwan Foundation. Ridhwan teachers are also ministers of the Ridhwan Foundation. They are trained by the DHAT Institute, the educational arm of the Ridhwan Foundation, through an extensive seven-year program, which is in addition to their work and participation as students of the Diamond Approach. The ordination process ensures that each person has a good working understanding of the Diamond Approach and a sufficient capacity to teach it before being ordained and authorized to be a Ridhwan teacher.

The Diamond Approach described in this book is taught in group and private settings in the United States, Canada, Europe, and Australia by Ridhwan teachers. For information about the various contexts for pursuing this work, we invite you to visit www.ridhwan.org. If you would like to explore starting a group in your area to be taught by ordained Ridhwan teachers, write:

Ridhwan
P.O. Box 2747
Berkeley, California 94702-0747

For more information on the books of A. H. Almaas, go to www.ahalmaas.com.

DIAMOND APPROACH and RIDHWAN are trademarks or registered trademarks of the Ridhwan Foundation.

Index